This book is
personally dedicated to

by

Malcolm C Barker
with best wishes ——— OCT 07 ———

a special edition from

GREAT NORTHERN

ESSENCE OF THE
YORKSHIRE COAST

Malcolm Barker

GREAT NORTHERN

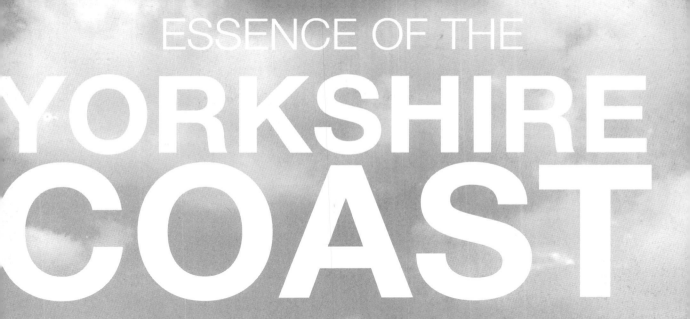

ESSENCE OF THE
YORKSHIRE
COAST

Malcolm Barker

To Dorothea and Patrick.

Great Northern Books Limited
PO Box 213, Ilkley, LS29 9WS
www.greatnorthernbooks.co.uk

ISBN: 978 1 905080 39 7

Design and layout: David Burrill

Printed in Spain

CIP Data
A catalogue for this book is available from the British Library

CONTENTS

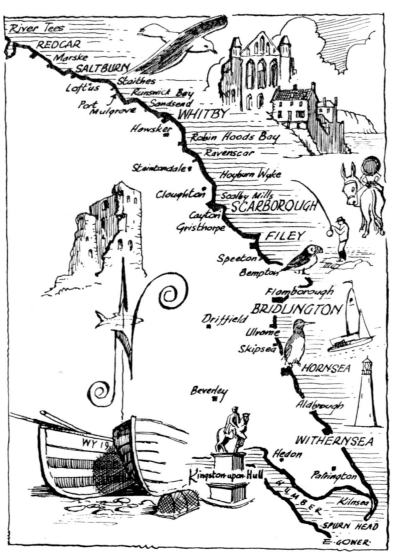

drawn by E. Gower

INTRODUCTION

THE Yorkshire coast stretches from the workaday lower reaches of the Tees to the mighty Humber, which drains one-sixth of England. It is a wonderful frontier for the county, offering great variety, from the cliffs at Boulby, 666ft above the sea, to the flat shore of Holderness. The level expanse of sand at Redcar contrasts with the rocky promontory of Filey Brigg.

It is redolent with history. Early man was there, leaving memorials such as the strange carved stone recently uncovered on Brow Moor, above Ravenscar, and Danes Dyke, a defensive earthwork across the headland at Flamborough. This huge undertaking was dug to a depth of 18ft, perhaps in the Iron Age, and is now a Scheduled Ancient Monument.

For centuries, anxious eyes scanned to seaward, watching for raiders. The Romans set up coastal signal stations that were intended to alert their inland encampments to the threat of invasion. The sites of several have been identified. At Huntcliffe, near Saltburn, the garrison may have come to grief, because excavations in 1911 revealed 14 skeletons in a well, all bearing evidence of having being knocked on the head. The Picts and the Scots came, and then the Anglo-Saxons, followed by the Vikings, prowling the coast and estuaries in their long ships, sacking, looting and burning.

Alcuin (737-804), a scholar who was born in York and became Master of the Cloister School, wrote: "It is 350 years that we and our fathers have inhabited this lovely land, and never before has such a terror appeared in Britain as we have now suffered from a pagan race, nor was it thought that such an inroad from the sea could be made."

It seems from this that Alcuin believed that his ancestors had arrived in England in a wave of Anglo-Saxon invasions that reached its third and final stage in 570 AD. He was undoubtedly complaining about a succession of Viking raids that began in about 793 when the monastery at Lindisfarne was plundered. Later St Hilda's Abbey at Whitby was destroyed, and its monks either fled or were slaughtered.

These invasions brought the transfusions of Teutonic and Nordic blood that pulse through the veins of our island race, and gave Yorkshire many of its place names. The Ridings themselves are owed to the Danes who took York in 857 AD, and conquered the Kingdom of Deira that extended south from the Tees and conformed more or less to the area we now know as Yorkshire. The Danes, under their leader Healfdene, seem to have been intent on colonisation, and within a decade they had parcelled the land into Ridings, a term derived from Old Norse meaning "third". These were to last 1,000 years until obliterated under the Conservative Government of Edward Heath in 1974.

The Normans came, building a great castle at Scarborough, and a new Abbey at Whitby. The Conquest eventually brought an increase in trade, with wool from such monastic flocks as those of Fountains and Rievaulx being exported to the Low Countries through Hull. Fishing developed into a major industry, with both Hull and Whitby sending whalers to the Arctic.

The Industrial Revolution added impetus, with the industrial towns offering new and reliable markets. Fleets from as far away as Cornwall and Scotland based themselves on harbours at Whitby, Scarborough and Bridlington during the herring season. On a single day in August 1868,

212 truckloads of fish passed through Malton on special trains, 135 from Scarborough and the rest from Whitby.

Eventually the North Sea came to be associated with pleasure. Scarborough had bathing machines in 1735 and by the end of the 18th Century the word "seaside" was being used in its present sense. The developing resorts did not rely merely on offering visitors sea-bathing, Scarborough, for instance, developing as a spa, and *A Trip to Scarborough*, a play by Richard Brinsley Sheridan (1751-1816), affords an insight into the style of the resort at that time.

One of the characters, Lord Foppington, exclaims: "Well, 'tis an unspeakable pleasure to be a man of quality – strike me dumb. Even the boors of this northern spa have learned the respect due to a title."

The Scarborians may have clutched their forelocks, but they extended their free hand for the money. Hutton's quaint *The Scarborough Tour*, published in 1803, contains the information: "All the visitants are dignified by the common people here with the name of 'Spaws'; all are obliged to pay 7s 6d during their abode, or not taste the water."

Coastal towns lacking the advantage of a spa claimed that simply breathing their air was likely to be beneficial. A mid-19th Century Redcar guide declared: "As a general stimulant, as a restorer of nervous energy, Sea Air possesses powers and properties superior to any other."

The Yorkshire coast has an unruly neighbour in the North Sea. It has been credited with some of the characteristics of a sentient being. Often ill-tempered, malevolent even, with huge breakers threatening to pluck unwary onlookers from exposed promenades, it also has periods of friendly calm, when desultory wavelets flop idly on the shore.

It has been sailed commercially since the Bronze Age, when cargoes of Irish gold and copper were despatched to the Continent, and as time passed it became a super-highway, with countless vessels engaged in the coasting trade. In the 19th Century, the volume of shipping increased rapidly, with a greater and greater demand in London and the south of England for coal shipped from the Tyne, Hartlepool and the new port of Middlesbrough on the Tees.

Some of the craft pressed into service for this profitable trade were of extraordinary antiquity. When the *Happy Return* of Whitby, laden with coal, was dashed to pieces on the Herdsand at the mouth of the Tyne in 1811, after the North Shields lifeboat *Northumberland* had taken off her crew, it was reported that she was 130 years old.

Another veteran whose ancient timbers shuttled between Tyne and Thames was the *Betsy Cairns*. She was driven on to rocks near Tynemouth in 1827, and became a total loss. There ensued a great scramble for fragments from the wreck, for it was widely believed that this was the vessel that had brought Prince William of Orange to England in the Glorious Revolution of 1688. Orange Lodges throughout the country requested souvenirs, and each member of Newcastle Corporation was presented with a snuffbox made from her timbers. Sadly, all the excitement proved unjustified, for the poet and historian Thomas Babington Macaulay (later the 1st Baron Macaulay), who was an accepted authority on the rule of William and Mary, pointed out that William III arrived in Torbay to challenge his father-in-law, James II, in a warship called *Brill*.

However, *Betsy Cairns* was remarkable in her own right, for Lloyds Register revealed that she had been built in 1690. For a number of years she served as a Royal yacht to successive monarchs, and later engaged in the West Indies trade before ending her days as a Tyne collier. Her timbers included some fine oak, richly and profusely carved, which had aged well, and was as black as ebony.

The *Remembrance*, a brig owned in Whitby, was built in Middlesbrough in 1862, and did not come to grief until 1904, when she foundered off the Suffolk coast, casting her old timbers and a cargo of coal destined for Greenwich on Bawdsey Sand. "Crew got to Harwich", records Richard Weatherill in his *Whitby and its Shipping*.

With great numbers of sailing ships flocking down the seaways at the mercy of wind and tide, some old, some ill-found, some ill-manned, it is perhaps not surprising that from time to time the North Sea shore became scattered with wrecks. Certain periods were worse than others. For example, 1861 was not merely a bad year in the history of the Yorkshire coast, but *the* bad year. It blew itself in with storms at New Year, and shrieked itself out in widows' weeds in December. In 12 months, no fewer than 778 vessels were flung up as wrecks against that wicked lee shore, the east coast.

The Board of Trade counted the cost: total vessels lost round Britain's coasts – 1,171; cost in lives – at least 465; lives saved by the pulling lifeboats – 743. In the appalling February of that year, 355 little ships were lost, many off the Yorkshire coast.

Most were the victims of one storm of the utmost ferocity. On 6th February a warning: "Caution – gale threatening from the north west, then northward", was telegraphed to major ports and communicated to shipping by signals. But the captains of the coasters put to sea: at least 100 left the Tyne and as many again sailed from neighbouring ports. Within two days, the timbers of this reckless armada littered the Yorkshire shore. Some ships simply disappeared, others were beaten to pieces on rocks, and some had their masts plucked out of them and sank. Rowing lifeboats attempted rescues, and it was on 9th February that the Whitby lifeboat capsized with the loss of 12 crewmen, plunging the town into mourning.

The crews of the colliers lived hard lives even in times when they were not in dire peril from the sea. Captain AH Rasmussen, who was born in Norway, recalled his first experience as a merchant seaman in his book *Sea Fever*, published in 1952. As a lad of 14 he went to South Shields intent on a life at sea, and joined the brigantine *Caroline* of Whitby*, laden with coals for Ipswich. He was given the job of ship's cook, and when he told the captain, a bluff Yorkshireman, that he had no experience, he was assured: "Tha's nowt to cook – tha's only to boil duff and beef."

The meat was so fat that Rasmussen could not bear to look at it, much less eat it. All week it was boiled salt beef (known as salt horse) followed by duff, and on Sundays, a boiled fresh joint, and duff with a few raisins scattered in it, thereby raising it to the status of plum duff. *Caroline*, he learned, was known as a hungry ship.

At the time he wrote the book Capt Rasmussen was looking back fifty years or more, to the beginning of the 20th Century, so *Caroline* must have been among the last collier brigs, sail having largely succumbed to steam by then.

His experience of frugal fare is a reminder of the canny way in which shipowners looked after

* *Capt Rasmussen may have changed the name of this vessel, for no* Caroline *is listed as being afloat at that time in* Whitby and its Shipping, *published by Richard Weatherill in 1908, and the autobiographer certainly gave a false name to another of his ships, for he wrote that he had done so.*

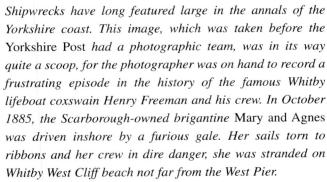

Shipwrecks have long featured large in the annals of the Yorkshire coast. This image, which was taken before the Yorkshire Post *had a photographic team, was in its way quite a scoop, for the photographer was on hand to record a frustrating episode in the history of the famous Whitby lifeboat coxswain Henry Freeman and his crew. In October 1885, the Scarborough-owned brigantine* Mary and Agnes *was driven inshore by a furious gale. Her sails torn to ribbons and her crew in dire danger, she was stranded on Whitby West Cliff beach not far from the West Pier.*

Freeman took the RNLI lifeboat Robert *and* Mary Ellis *to sea, but in trying to get alongside the wreck he overshot, and the would-be rescuers found themselves beached and unable to help, despite desperate attempts to re-launch their boat. After two oars snapped, onlookers rushed into the sea to try to push her off. The lifeboat can be seen in the foreground, with what may be her crew alongside.*

No doubt this embarrassing state of affairs was viewed by large crowds, and it was fortunate for the crew of the Mary and Agnes *that the Whitby Rocket Brigade got a line across, and drew them to safety through the surf. As the lightest aboard, the ship's apprentice was sent first to test the line, and then one by one the others braved the raging sea.*

Henry Freeman eventually retired from the lifeboat service in 1899, an event marked by a rare tribute, a special supplement in the Whitby Gazette. *He was credited with helping to save more than 300 lives during his time with the lifeboats. The poor* Mary and Agnes *was described as a "fine ship", but she did not survive the stranding, and was knocked down within a week for a mere £11.*

Frank Meadow Sutcliffe, the Whitby photographer, took a similar picture that day. What he could not convey was the sheer ferocity of the wind. He recalled later that it was so strong that he was unable to walk, "all one could do was crawl along on all fours." To obtain his picture he needed assistance from "a big heavy soldier, an artillery man, who was on the beach at the time, who curled himself up under the tripod and held on with two hands to the two legs which caught the most wind. Without that help, it would have been impossible to have done anything."

A more recent shipwreck. An old Greek steamer, the 4,200-ton Taxiarchis, *lies stranded off Redcar in May 1952, and according to the original caption was in the process of being broken up. She went ashore on 14 January that year, and must have been considered too old and decrepit to make re-floating worthwhile.*

their interests. Robert Barry succeeded as head of the shipping company JH Barry, of Whitby and Bishopgate, London, on the death of his father in 1826. He figures in a couple of books written by a retired Scarborough headmaster, John Howard, *Bound for Van Dieman's Land* (North Yorkshire County Record Office, 1996) and *Master Mariner Extraordinary* (Regional Studies Series, 1995).

The captains encountered in these books, William Mintoft Maw of Scarborough, and Edward Theaker of Staithes, were both employed by Robert Barry.

He is in the background, a bit player compared with the sailors, perhaps, but he nevertheless threatens to steal the show, for his conduct of JH Barry and Co evokes a composite character from Dickens, with a nice dash of Scrooge injected into that eminently practical man of business, Thomas Gradgrind of Coketown. There is an awful fascination to be derived from glimpses of Barry at work, however fleeting.

His pursuit of the errant penny was relentless. After studying accounts for provisions for Capt Maw's *Gilmore*, he wrote succinctly to her master, noting that he had been charged for two potato sacks and a basket. He would thank Capt Maw to "ask the steward what became of them".

Mr Howard commented: "The owner of a fleet of vessels trading with the uttermost ends of the earth who, from his shipping office in the City of London, wrote concerning the fate of two potato sacks and a basket, deserves every success".

The meticulous instruction emanating from the counting-house extended to water butts used for storage on the outward voyage. Capt Maw could sell them at Sydney or Hobart, depending where he could get the better price. Otherwise, he could try Colombo, where Mr Barry gathered that large butts were in demand for the export of coconut oil.

On that voyage, Capt Maw embarked 254 involuntary passengers from convict hulks and landed them in Hobart 130 days after clearing Sheerness. He returned with nine fare-paying passengers, and a cargo of wool, tallow, bark and tar.

The shipping business Robert Barry nurtured so assiduously eventually burgeoned into a fleet of tramp steamers, but their black, white and red funnels disappeared from the high seas in 1913 when the last of them was sold.

Robert Barry died in 1870. Subsequently a degree of frivolity appeared to have afflicted the family, finding its most outrageous expression on the family estate at Fyling Hall, near Robin Hood's Bay, where his successor, John Warren Barry, built a pigsty in the form of a classical temple.

For all its awesome reputation, the North Sea is little more than a boisterous puddle in comparison with the major oceans. In its present form, a crude funnel-shape, it is in its youth. Less than 10,000 years ago, which is yesterday in geological terms, the Dogger Bank was a peat moor. The Straits of Dover only opened up some 7,000 years ago, and are so shallow that Patrington church's famous spire would broach the waves at the deepest part.

Despite sea-borne raids by the Germans in 1914, during which Scarborough and Whitby were shelled, the North Sea has rightly been regarded in this country as a grey moat across which foreign foes could only glower.

Overall, the coast is a very special part of Yorkshire. Its remarkable variations mean that it is never dull, and mostly picturesque. Even Holderness has its charms, though it is not the real coast, but merely the debris dumped during and immediately after a period of glaciation. The real coast, the White Cliffs of Yorkshire, run inland, and are buried under the flank of the East Riding Wolds. Holderness is gradually vanishing, and perhaps waves are destined to beat once more on those White Cliffs. According to one reckoning, Holderness's muddy seaward edge is receding at six ft and more a year. Since the early Middle Ages between 20 and 30 towns, villages and smaller settlements have slipped into the sea, giving rise to strange tales of church bells heard tolling beneath the waves.

A village that disappeared during the 19th Century was Outhorne or Owthorne, north of Withernsea. In 1822, it consisted of a church and 12 houses. John Phillips, later Professor of Geology at Oxford University, visited it in 1828, when only one tombstone remained in the churchyard, bearing an inscription implying the expectation of the deceased that he must lay there till Christ should appear. A few years later the burial ground was lost to the sea, and by 1909 no trace of the village remained. Owthorne Mere, a freshwater lake like Hornsea Mere, was also engulfed.

Yorkshire's more stable cliffs have yielded wealth in the form of alum, jet and ironstone. Its Cretaceous and Jurassic rocks have provided fossilised evidence of distant times, including an abundance of ammonites, which became extinct 65m years ago. Reptilian recoveries include Ichthyosaurus, a kind of fish-lizard, and Plesiosaurus, which, with its nasty looking teeth and long neck, resembled everybody's idea of the Loch Ness Monster. Fossils of both these creatures are carefully preserved in the Whitby Literary and Philosophical Museum.

This book seeks to explore some of the many aspects of the coast, beginning at the top, at the mouth of the Tees.

AT THE MOUTH OF THE TEES

THE South Gare breakwater, Yorkshire's most northerly seaward extension, is in complete contrast to Spurn Point at the opposite extremity, being entirely man-made. It is an astonishing structure, two-and-a-half miles in length, and it had been a quarter of a century in the building when it was officially opened in 1888.

Basically it is an enormous slagheap deposited horizontally instead of vertically. With its companion, North Gare, which extends from the County Durham shore, it enables the Tees Conservancy Commissioners to provide a safe deep-water entrance from the North Sea, or the German Ocean, as it was once known, to the dockyards and wharves of Middlesbrough. The terms North and South Gare were originally applied to sandbanks flanking the Tees estuary. Variations in wind and tides caused them to shift constantly, thus altering the course of the main channel, which was shallow at low tide, perhaps no more than a couple of feet deep.

Shipping to and from Stockton, ten miles upstream and then the river's principal port, had to brave this hazardous bar. Steps were taken to "alter, widen and deepen" the channel in 1805, but as late as 1830 Whitby harbour, stinking with sewage, silted up, and with a dangerous entry, was reckoned superior to anything on the Tees or, indeed, the Tyne. The Stockton and Darlington Railway, built to carry coals from the pits of south-west Durham to the sea, had been opened in 1825, but so bad was the navigation below Stockton that the line was carried on to Middlesbrough, then a hamlet of 154 people, by 1930.

The first dock was opened in 1841 when Port Darlington, as it was sometime called, had grown to a town of 5,500 people. Its first house was built by George Chapman, a joiner, in West Street in 1830, and bore a plaque to that effect until it was demolished in 1960. Chapman went on to build

The lighthouse on South Gare, the great breakwater that guards the mouth of the Tees.

a house for himself in Dacre Street, and his son, John Richard, born on 22nd August 1830, was the new town's first child.

A distance inland from the mouth of the Tees are the Eston Hills, an outlier of the Cleveland Hills, which provided a fair proportion of the material from which South Gare was built. This came about after a June day in 1850 when two gentlemen, Mr John Vaughan and Mr John Marley, exploring the slopes of Eston Nab, to the northerly end of the Hills, beheld to their delight and astonishment that a layer of ironstone fully 16ft thick had been laid bare in a quarry from which stone had been taken for roads.

It was no fortuitous discovery. Both men were well aware that seams of ironstone ran through the Cleveland Hills. Marley was a mining engineer and geologist who thought trial borings might be worthwhile on the Nab. Vaughan and his partner Henry Bolckow had blast furnaces for which they obtained ironstone from a royalty at Grosmont in the Esk Valley owned by Mrs Clark (daughter of the great whaling captain William Scoresby).

The ladies are holding their hats as they take a ride on the sail-powered bogey on the rail track along South Gare.

This raw material had to be shipped from Whitby, a vexatious business according to Joseph Bewick in his *Cleveland Ironstone* (1859) due to "the wretched condition of the harbour at Whitby, which is so much silted up with mud and other debris, that no ship of any size can leave the port with a full cargo."

Therefore John Vaughan could probably hardly believe his luck that June day when he beheld a seam of ironstone of hitherto unprecedented thickness virtually on the doorstep of the foundry he had set up in Middlesbrough with Henry Bolckow. He was even luckier then he knew, for around the time he and Marley were taking their momentous stroll, Henry Bessemer was perfecting his new steel-making process. The Cleveland ore contained too much phosphorus for his discovery to be applied on Teesside, but two cousins, Gilchrist Thomas and Percy Gilchrist, who had been experimenting at Blaenavon in Wales, overcame this difficulty. They read a paper on their work at the 1879 meeting of the Iron and Steel Institute. Bolckow's directors had been following their progress with interest, and invited them to put their ideas into practice at Eston. The upshot was that Middlesbrough was soon making steel of a quality that matched any in the world.

Back in 1850, Bolckow and Vaughan had wasted no time. In September, only three months after the discovery, Eston sent a load of seven tons of ore for smelting, a dribble, perhaps, but the forerunner of a cataract. During 1851 nearly 200,000 tons were dug out and five years later output was between 10,000 and 20,000 tons a week. By 1841 Middlesbrough had 41 blast furnaces, and

A busy dockside scene at Middlesbrough in July 1979 justifies the claim made by Sir Hugh Bell, chairman of the Tees Conservancy Commissioners from 1903 to 1931, that they had converted a mountain stream into a great port.

was girdling the world with its iron rails. Its population was then 18,700

Eston endowed men with wealth and prestige. Marley left £500,000, a phenomenal sum in those days, Bolckow became the new Borough of Middlesbrough's first Mayor when the booming town was granted incorporation in 1853, and Vaughan had his portrait hung in the Council Chamber and his statue put up in the town

The ironmasters, once neighbours in Cleveland Street, soon housed themselves more grandly, Bolckow at Marton Hall and Vaughan at Gunnergate Hall.

The residue of their processing of the ironstone from Eston and other mines was a vast quantity of slag, and it was this material that the Tees Conservancy Commissioners used for their breakwater. They also charged the ironmasters a copper or two for each ton removed, which must have been perceived as a good deal all round, as among the Commissioners were none other than Messrs Bolckow and Vaughan. Exporting their wares was crucial to their success, hence their interest in the river. Well into the 20th Century more then half of the cargo shipped out of the Tees was classed as iron and steel goods.

Further impetus for the provision of a safe entry to the Tees was provided by the great storm of February 1861, which strewed the east coast with wrecks, including the loss of between 50 to 60 vessels within sight of Hartlepool and Tees Bay. The construction of South Gare was approved by Act of Parliament, and the first stone was laid in November 1863. According to William Lillie (*The History of Middlesbrough*, 1968) the quantity of slag deposited by 1877 was 3,255,356 tons. Its effect was to ensure a depth of water on the Middle Ground, as the Teesmouth bar is called, of 20ft at low water. Another benefit was the establishment of a Harbour of Refuge for vessels caught offshore by stormy weather.

The breakwater also contributed vastly to the development of Middlesbrough as a port. Prior to its construction, there were only two or three feet of water on the bar at low tide. A lighthouse 43ft high was provided at its head, and a pilot station to landward.

The Gare, together with other works undertaken by the Commissioners, enabled Sir Hugh Bell, chairman from 1903 to 1931, to declare: "The Tees is a peculiar river. It is a mountain stream which we have converted into a great port. For a little over a million pounds we have got one of the most remarkable ports in the country."

The breakwater's slag base was given a concrete cover, and a tramway carried visitors along its entire length on a curious contrivance called a sail bogey. A postcard shows this as a box-like seat mounted on a flat cart that ran on four iron wheels. It carried a triangular sail, and two women in long white dresses are shown clinging anxiously to their hats as they prepare to be propelled by wind-power, which is rarely lacking on the Gare.

Eston Nab broods over the river mouth and the industrial landscape of Teesside, to which it made so vast a contribution. Its summit is a curious place seamed by tracks and scarred by gullies and hollows. Early man was there, leaving behind fragments of flint. Later, occupants of the Eston Hills created a fortress on an impressive scale. Guarded to the north by an escarpment, it is surrounded on the other three sides by a rampart and an outer fosse some 350 yards in circumference.

The reason for these huge earthworks is lost in pre-history. But the mute evidence of laborious work by many hands speaks of fear, of invasion, perhaps, or raiders from the north. From 800ft above sea level the occupants had a wonderful vantage point. By a sweep of their eyes, they were able to keep a watch on the Tees estuary, and the Durham shore. On the far horizon, rising like battlements, they could discern the Cheviots and the mountains of Cumberland and Westmoreland. Later, much later, a beacon tower was built on the Nab. Again, its erection was prompted by fear, this time of attack during the Napoleonic Wars. A monument put up in 1956 now marks its site.

The Eston Hills are riddled with disused ironstone workings. According to one estimate, they yielded 165m tons of stone by the time the last mine closed in 1949. This was the bedrock on which the prosperity of Middlesbrough was built, and now Eston Nab, its surface riven and its interior plundered, provides a splendid platform from which to contemplate the industrial landscape it helped create.

It's earlier character as a viewpoint is conveyed in the second edition of a guide to Redcar, published in 1852:

"From Eston Nab, a most splendid and extensive prospect meets the eye, embracing all that is sublime and picturesque. From hence when the atmosphere is clear and the sky cloudless (may be seen) the most enchanting panorama of which any land could boast."

By then, of course, Messrs Marley and Vaughan had made their discovery. Even now, more than 150 years on, visitors might have a long wait before the atmosphere over Teesside could again be classified as clear.

CHARLES HALL, HERO OF STOKESLEY

ON the 22nd June 1940, the day France submitted to Hitler's armistice terms, a newly-built corvette that had been intended for the French Navy, *La Bastiase*, was on trial in Tees Bay when she was torn apart by an explosion, and sank within minutes. Only about a dozen of the 72 souls on board survived, and the dead included members of the staff of the shipbuilder, Smith's Dock, of South Bank, Middlesbrough.

News of the disaster, believed to have been caused by a mine but never fully explained, was suppressed, for the very existence of corvettes was a closely-guarded secret. They were being hastily constructed to counter the U-Boat threat, and a naval designer based them on a whale-catcher built at Smith's Dock, the *Southern Pride*.

The *La Bastiase* disaster apart, good progress with the new warships was being made at the yard in 1940. The little ships were called Flower Class corvettes by the Royal Navy, and a roll call of those launched on the Tees that year sounds like a catalogue of plants for a cottage garden: *Tulip, Verbena, Gladiolus, Godetia* and *Stonecrop*. Another which was approaching completion at the time of the *La Bastiase* explosion had, like her, been intended for the French. However, by the time she was launched on 4th July 1940 she was *HMS Nasturtium*, and on 27th June 1941 she distinguished herself off Iceland in partnership with *Gladiolus and Celandine* by destroying U-566 with depth charges.

Corvettes were originally intended for the protection of coastal convoys, but their seagoing qualities and long range enabled them to play a vital role in the early stages of the Battle of the Atlantic, as dramatically described by Nicholas Monsarrat in his book *The Cruel Sea*, which featured a corvette, *Compass Rose*. *

They were of simple design, and parts common to merchant shipping went into their construction, which meant they could be produced from many small shipyards. Eventually 267 of them, built in Canada as well as Britain, went into service. They were reckoned to be cold, and to roll alarmingly in heavy seas, but they were very seaworthy, and in addition to helping the convoys get through they took a toll of U-Boats, maybe 47 in all.

Among those who perished that June day in Tees Bay was a remarkable man called Charles William Hall, who was on the Smith's Dock design team as an engineering draughtsman. He volunteered under-age for the Army in the First World War, and was with the Royal Engineers at the Somme in 1916 and Cambrai and Passchendaele in 1917. His sister Marion proudly recalled that his comrades knew him as "the bravest lad we have ever seen". On 5th September 1918, with the end of the war little more than a month away, he was stepping out of a train on his return to the front after a spell in hospital when a shell hit the station, and he was so severely wounded that his leg had to be amputated below the knee.

He got around nimbly enough on his wooden leg, and despite his disability insisted on sailing with *La Bastiase* when she went on trial with her French crew, taking the place of a colleague who was best man at a wedding that day. Thus, having been maimed in one war, Charles Hall was killed in the next.

The ships he had worked on were destined to help win the Battle of the Atlantic, but that could not have been foreseen by his friends and family in 1940. They were obliged to mourn him without being able to proclaim that he had died in the service of his country, so strict was the censorship. Several senior staff at Smith's Dock were lost with him, but the Middlesbrough *Evening Gazette* had to stagger the obituary announcements over several days for fear their simultaneous appearance might enable the enemy to deduce that a catastrophe had struck the town.

Inability to proclaim their heroism may have seemed particularly ironic in the case of Charles Hall, for nobody had done more than he to ensure that the deeds and sacrifice of the fallen of the First World War were properly recorded. He lived at Stokesley, where, in the Parish Church of St Peter and St Paul, is preserved the Book of Remembrance that he created as a memorial to his fellow townsmen.

Photographs of each man appear on left-hand pages. Opposite, set out in immaculate copperplate hand, are brief biographies, and, as far as they were available, details of how they met their deaths.

This is impressive enough, but the book is made truly extraordinary by the way the pages are illuminated. The text throughout is bordered by representations of flowers and country scenes, all in glowing colours, and with no page like another. It is as though Charles Hall was trying to convey the visions of home the men had treasured before being doomed to lie forever in a foreign land. There are the buttercup meadows of their youth, the stands of trees, the drifts of bluebells, the riverbank willows, the cottage gardens, and the distant glimpses of the Cleveland Hills.

Charles William Hall's courage and self-sacrifice of 1940 were eventually given public acknowledgement, and his name is on the War Memorial in the church, mounted on the wall above the Book of Remembrance, in which he recorded 57 fallen comrades of an earlier war.

In 1999 he received further recognition when the Stokesley Society published *A Stokesley Diary* that he had kept since 1901, noting down local happenings he thought of interest, and some national events. His sister Marion maintained this record until she died in 1971, so the diary begins with Queen Victoria's death and ends with the change to decimal currency.

* HMS Compass Rose *was played in the film of Monsarrat's book* The Cruel Sea *by HMS Coreopsis, built by A & J Inglis Ltd of Glasgow and launched on 23rd April 1940. For a time during her service she flew the flag of the Royal Hellenic Navy.*

THE RAILWAY RESORTS

EDWARD Baines published his monumental *Yorkshire*, a kind of roll-call of the county, in two volumes in 1822 and 1823, He said of Saltburn that it was "inhabited chiefly by fishermen", Withernsea was "a small village" with ten farmers and two shoemakers, Hornsea had lost its market but was "much frequented in the bathing season".

This last comment gives a clue to the factor uniting the small communities situated at the extremities of the Yorkshire coast. By the end of the century, due entirely to the coming of railways, they had grown into holiday resorts.

SALTBURN has the uncommon distinction of being inspired by a vision. In 1859 Henry Pease told his wife that as he rested on a hillside above the old fishing hamlet of Saltburn, he saw a town arise on the cliffs before him. At the time, he was probably staying with his brother Joseph, who owned the imposing Cliff House at Marske. As a son of Edward Pease, the wealthy Quaker industrialist, and a shrewd businessman himself, Henry had the wherewithal to make his dream reality.

He persuaded fellow directors of the Stockton and Darlington Railway to implement an Act of Parliament of 1858 that authorised the extension of their line to Saltburn. He formed the Saltburn Improvement Company, and in 1861 laid the foundation stone of the new holiday resort's first house. To ensure harmony, he required that roofs were to be of Westmoreland slate and all frontages were to be of white firebricks, which, happily, were readily available from a Pease brickworks. Other regulations specified streets where dormer windows were permitted. Building plots were sold, and to ensure purchasers got on with the job, the Improvement Company insisted that sites would be forfeit if construction was not finished within two years.

If a similar rule had been enforced at Ravenscar, near Robin Hood's Bay, where another attempt was made to create a new town, it might have been completed. Its fate was to remain a mere shadow, with a few villas, some shops, a railway station, a church and many empty sites, the inheritors of which were still turning up in search of their properties in the 1970s.

By the time Henry Pease died in 1881, Saltburn was a fashionable resort. A Dr Stainthorpe proclaimed its death rate the lowest of any watering place in the country.

John Bell, a wealthy ironmaster, chose it as the site for his magnificent Rushpool Hall, which cost £100,000 and was reckoned to be one of the most splendid houses in the north-east. His family firm was Bell Brothers, which in 1899 possessed a dozen furnaces, wharves on the Tees at Middlesbrough, coal and ironstone mines, and 1,000 cottages. In that year it merged with Dorman Long.

Rushpool Hall contained an ornate ballroom, a staircase of Italian marble, and, a rarity in those days, a covered swimming pool, where the Prince of Wales was said to have disported himself during a stay with the Bells.

One of the Bells' maids, Eleanor Swalwell, was an early exponent of photography, and assembled an album of pictures of Rushpool Hall and its inhabitants, which was fortunate because

This postcard shows Saltburn's newly-restored pier, and the cliff railway.

a fire reduced it to a smoke-blackened shell in 1904. Young Eleanor's photographs show a bizarre structure with two towers, one circular and the other square, and massive walls of main-seam Cleveland ironstone, dug, presumably, from the Bell Brothers' Normanby mines.

Its principal architectural rival in the new town was the Zetland Hotel, an Italianate structure with an imposing central tower. Guests travelling by rail arrived at a special platform that was virtually part of the hotel, only a few paces from the reception area.

Saltburn also had colourful public gardens complete with their own Albert Memorial, successfully metamorphosed from its original role as the portico of Barnard Castle railway station. From 1884, twin saloons of an inclined tramway, impelled ingeniously by water, provided transport up and down the cliffs. Near the lower terminus were a pier, a promenade, and a beautiful beach. Brine baths offered contents said to be "ten time stronger than sea water".

The pier, which opened in 1869, was the first in the north-east to be made of iron. The designer, a railway contractor, John Anderson, presumably adhered to the material. he knew best. It was a huge success, with 60,000 people walking its 1,400ft length in the first year, but it has since been knocked about by the North Sea, with the latest major repairs being carried out in 2000/2001.

What would Henry Pease make of his vision today? Some of the streets he named proudly after jewels, Emerald, Pearl, Garnet and so on, are sadly tarnished. Former private hotels on the Marine Parade are flats. Rushpool Hall became a hotel. The Zetland is apartments, and its access by train was abandoned in 1970. The railway station of 1860/61, the very core of the town, had a classical façade and a large circular booking hall. It is now shops, and trains have been banished to an outside platform. Some quite hideous post-war commercial development defaces the centre.

Nevertheless, Henry Pease's masterpiece of town planning may still be admired, and a visitor will readily understand why Saltburn's magnificent location so excited its begetter that he was quite out of breath when he got home to tell his wife about his cliff-top vision.

WITHERNSEA's population at the 1851 census was 109, but it was soon to undergo a sudden influx. The Hull and Holderness Railway, which initially connected it with Victoria Dock in Hull, and later the city's Paragon Station, was opened on 27th June 1854 amid much rejoicing and general acclaim, for no fewer than 63,000 travelled from Hull that summer. For the folk of the great city, the era of the day trip had well and truly arrived.

Withernsea is a curious and interesting place. In 1877 an organisation with the catchall title of Withernsea Pier, Promenade, Gas and General Improvement Company put up a 1,196ft pier. It was much buffeted by the tides, and in a great gale of October 1880, suffered the indignity of being split in two by a storm-swept coal barge, the *Saffron*. It was rebuilt, but on March 28th 1882 big seas swept away the pier-head and it saloon. There were other mishaps until, in 1903, all that remained was a stump. This remnant was removed, but the imposing pier entrance, with two large towers and two small, remains, and has been refurbished. This bizarre structure is said to have been inspired by Conway Castle, and if so it was a pleasant whimsy to challenge the North Sea with a replica of Welsh battlements.

There is also an old lighthouse where the keeper had the privilege, rare in his trade, of sharing the accommodation with his wife. The light maintained by this homely pair last shone in 1976, and the 127ft structure now houses memorabilia associated with the actress Kay Kendall, who was born in Withernsea.

Also worthy of commemoration is Anthony Bannister, an Alderman of Kingston-upon-Hull, who, as first chairman of the Railway Company, had high hopes of making Withernsea a fashionable resort, and engaged Cuthbert Brodrick as architect. He designed the town station and the Queen's Hotel, advertised as being "unsurpassed by any other hotel on the coast", but after it failed to pay its way Sir James Reckitt and his brother Francis bought it, and gave it to Hull Royal Infirmary as a convalescent home. Brodrick also planned an estate of broad streets and elegant terraces, but little building took place, and having one of the streets that were laid out named in his honour must have been small consolation to Ald Bannister.

His railway had a short independent life, being taken over by the North Eastern Railway. It succumbed to the Beeching axe in 1964.

Modern Withernsea is a dormitory town for Hull, beset on one side by a sea intent on encroaching on the Holderness shore, and, from inland, a tidal wave of holiday caravans.

HORNSEA's answer to Anthony Bannister was Joseph Armytage Wade (1820-1893).

He, too, was first chairman of a railway company, which in his case was the Hull and Hornsea. Unlike Withernsea, which had been a mere hamlet, Hornsea was a busy little town attracting sea-bathers before he came on the scene, but his railway, opened in 1864, added impetus to its growth. He also provided employment by setting up the Hornsea Brick and Tile Works on a site later occupied by the Hornsea Pottery Company.

Examples of Wade's products are preserved at Hornsea's delightful North Holderness Museum of Village Life, housed in Burns Farm, Newbegin. There is also an unrivalled collection of Hornsea Pottery.

Joseph Armytage Wade's family interest in Hornsea was derived from his uncle, John Wade, a Hull timber merchant, who had a home there. A trend had developed in the early 19th Century for wealthy Hull businessmen to set themselves up at Hornsea after Thomas Collinson built the first of the town's handsome villas in 1802.

Joseph's many enterprises included a 1,072ft pier, opened in May 1880 and wrecked in October of that year during the same storm that resulted in similar havoc at Withernsea. It appears that the North Sea resents the intrusion of pleasure piers on its territory, and gives them short shrift. Nothing so grand as Withernsea's towers remains at Hornsea, although two stone lions in public gardens at Park Row guard a fragment of its pier.

Wade (1817-1896) was a godly man, funding non-conformist chapels and at the same time serving as a churchwarden at St Nicholas's, Hornsea's 15th Century parish church. He sought to shield possible sinners from temptation; in 1864 he was chairman of the local board that decreed that men's and women's bathing machines should be not less than 200 yards apart.

The rail link with Hull closed in 1964, but the station, built to a design by Rawlins Gould of York, survives, and is now used for housing.

WHEN LINGER'S GHOST WALKED – AND MANY RAN

SMUGGLER CAPTURED – A small smuggler, the *Goede Hoope*, of Ostend, laden with contraband goods, was brought into Whitby, having been captured by Lieutenant King, chief officer of the preventive service at Whitby, with three men and two pilots. The cargo consisted of about 300 kegs of spirits and tobacco, snuff, tea etc.

JUST as interesting as this brief news report from the Whitby Repository of June 1828 is the footnote that follows, which was apparently added at the request of the two pilots who accompanied the preventive men in their swoop on the smuggler, Jacob Coupland and Thomas Douglass.

There was apparently a belief in Whitby that they had alerted Lieut King to the presence offshore of the *Goede Hoope*. The editor of the Repository, "in justice to the pilots", declared there was no foundation to such stories and, prior to being required to accompany Lieut King, "they had seen nothing like a smuggler in the roads". The pilots were plainly anxious for their fellow townsfolk to know they were not informants, for such a reputation would have cost them dear on the Yorkshire coast, where smuggling, albeit against the law, was regarded by many as a legitimate occupation.

That attitude ran down from the topmost layer of society. In 1744 when Hamlet Woods was Collector of Customs for the Crown at Whitby, his masters in London wrote to him asking why known free-traders had not been prosecuted.

Woods, who had been at Whitby since 1717, replied that despite his repeated applications the Justices at Whitby "absolutely refused to give any penalties". The magistrates' explanation for their connivance at lawbreaking was ingenious. They said that when people were worth nothing, imprisonment cost the townsfolk money, for they had to maintain the felons' families during their incarceration.

The magistrates were formidable characters in the town, one of them none other than the Lord of the Manor himself, Hugh Cholmley. Despite the bench's forbearance, the preventive men did make some notable seizures. In two-and-a-half years, 1722-24, contraband intercepted in Whitby amounted to 306 half-ankers of spirits (a half anker was a Dutch measure equal to about four-and-a-quarter Imperial gallons) and an extraordinary catalogue of other items, including ten yards of muslin, eight handkerchiefs, and canisters of snuff and tea.

On October 16 1723, one of the Riding Officers who patrolled the coast on horseback made a seizure at Marske, near Loftus, listed as Spanish Juice (liquorice), iron wire, four flying jib booms, two spears, 12lbs of pepper, and many other articles.

These statistics were drawn from a summary of Whitby Customs documents going back 300

The Ship Inn at Saltburn was the reputed haunt of smugglers in olden times. This picture was taken in May 1952.

years that had been collated by Mr James Niven, who retired as the port's Customs and Excise Officer in 1948 after 27 years in the post. Access to Mr Niven's notes helped Mr John Tindale produce his book *Owlers, Hoverers and Revenuemen* (1986), owlers being exporters of contraband, mainly those who sent wool to the Continent in defiance of an Act of King Charles II. Those caught in breach of this law faced condign punishment, or so it would appear from this couplet in Brown's Collected Poems of 1798:

To Gibbets and Gallows your owlers advance,
That, that's the sure way to Mortify France.

The Oxford English Dictionary suggests that the term came into use because those shipping wool abroad worked nocturnally, like owls. The dictionary is no help with hoverers, but in Yorkshire it meant those who imported contraband, and were in the habit of lurking off shore until the coast was clear for a "run", quite literally hovering

Smugglers carried on their business over the whole length of the Yorkshire coast, not always furtively either. Some of the more resolute, whose daring made them folk-heroes, operated off Scarborough and Filey. George Stoney Fagg plied his heavily-armed schooner *Kent* between

Holland and various coves and inlets, bringing in French brandy, Geneva gin, Holland linen, tea and salt. In 1777, after encounters with revenue cutters off Robin Hood's Bay and Runswick, *Kent* was cornered off Filey. "Fire, you b-----s and be damned to you," roared Stoney Fagg. He was taken after a desperate battle in which his sailing master and four of his crew were killed.

At Saltburn, John Andrews, the licensee of the Ship Inn, was acknowledged "King of the Smugglers". He was part owner of a schooner called the *Morgan Rattler*, and when the word went out that "Andrews's cow has calved", helpers knew she lay off Saltburn with a cargo to unload.

The gang used an underground passage to store contraband, the entrance being under a flagstone in the stables, in the stall of a horse that lashed savagely if a stranger came within range.

Andrews made huge profits. For example, he was able to buy tea in Holland at seven pence a pound, against the cost in this country of anything from 12s to 35s. In 1746 a witness before a Parliamentary Commission estimated that of four million pounds weight of tea consumed in this country every year, three million pounds were smuggled.

Eventually Andrews left the Ship Inn to live at the White House, Saltburn, and continue his smuggling enterprises under the cover of being a successful farmer and businessman. He became the first President and Master of Foxhounds of the new Roxby and Cleveland Hunt. He also enrolled as an Ensign in the Cleveland Volunteers, demonstrating that he was a patriot even though he defrauded the King of his customs dues.

David "Smoker" Browning was another notorious smuggler. His aptly-named schooner *Porcupine* bristled with 14 carriage guns, four three-pounders, and a large number of smaller weapons. Thus armed, "Smoker" was quite ready to give battle. In 1788, he turned on the revenue cutter *Eagle* off Robin Hood's Bay, and sent her packing with her sails shot full of holes and her rigging in tatters. Browning was eventually taken by a Royal Navy vessel, HMS *Kite*, in the English Channel.

Once landed, contraband was quickly hidden pending transfer inland. At Robin Hood's Bay, it was said that so many of the cottages were connected by doors, passages or double cupboards that a bolt of silk could be passed from Wayfoot to Bank Top without emerging from cover. Hugh Kendall, who assembled information about smuggling that is now preserved in the library of Whitby Literary and Philosophical Society, reported that there was scarcely a dwelling in the old part of Bay Town that did not have a hiding hole of some kind.

As the pony trains assembled in Bay to take goods inland along the old moorland track leading to Saltersgate, villagers were encouraged to stay indoors, the more superstitious of them by threats that if they ventured out they might encounter an apparition known as "Linger's Ghost".

Another smugglers' road led inland from Loftus to Bilsdale. Cargoes landed at various points between Marske and Runswick Bay were hidden at Loftus Mill and delivered locally by the miller's wagon. To the south, Scarborough had a notorious smugglers' inn, The Three Mariners. It had 26 cupboards, some tiny, some with false floors. One of the larger upstairs cupboards connected with the next room. Rapid escape from the place would be easy, and a small staircase window is supposed to have served as a lookout.

Filey also had an inn supposed to be the haunt of free-traders, The Ship, and one of its ancient beams was hollowed out to make a hiding place. At one time the parish clerk at Hornsea is supposed to have acted as storekeeper for smugglers, and kept goods in the vaulted crypt beneath the parish church. One night in December 1732, a great gale blew up, lifting off the church roof and toppling the steeple. Below ground among his barrels, the clerk was said to have been so petrified by such heavenly wrath that he had a stroke, and never spoke again.

The beach at Barmston was used so frequently to "run" French brandy, even during the Napoleonic Wars, that villagers assumed the whole of France knew it as an excellent landing ground, including Napoleon's generals. Fears grew that the boots of an invading army would tread the sands one moonlit night, and took such a hold on the villagers' imagination that some prepared to evacuate Barmston, and a few actually went.

Such tales abound, and avoidance of what Dr Johnson called "the hateful tax of Customs and Excise" was at its peak in the 18th Century. But attitudes were changing, and the Whitby historian George Young, after commenting that Staithes, Robin Hood's Bay and Saltburn were "noted for smuggling", wrote in 1817 that "every friend of mankind will desire the complete suppression of a traffic as pernicious to the morals of all concerned in it as to the public revenue and the fair trader".

The formation of the Coastguard in 1822 strengthened the Government's arm. By the end of that decade, smuggling was in decline. Disciplined ex-Royal Navy men, battle-hardened during the Napoleonic Wars, were recruited to uphold the law, and, off-shore, warships patrolled the North Sea and English Channel, halting and searching vessels suspected of free-trading. Ships caught smuggling were broken up, and profit margins shrank as duties were reduced.

In 1827, the luck of "King" Andrews ran out at last. Caught red-handed at Hornsea, he was heavily fined. The £200,000 impost was beyond his means to pay, and he was imprisoned in York Castle. There he remained until powerful friends persuaded Lord Bexley, Chancellor of the Duchy of Lancaster, to grant him a reprieve.

This was a wonderful case of turning the other cheek. Before being raised to the Peerage, Lord Bexley was Nicholas Vansittart, Chancellor of the Exchequer, and therefore well aware of the losses to the Treasury caused by men like Andrews. The smuggler returned home an old man, and found the Coastguards in charge.

Thus, the ignominious end of the voyage of the *Goede Hoope*, recorded by the Whitby Repository in 1828, was one of the last episodes of a lawless and adventurous era on the Yorkshire coast.

'MAISTER' FIPS AND THE FISHERMEN

From time to time my contributions to the *Yorkshire Post* took the form of book reviews. I have chosen this one, written in 2006, because it features an old friend and schoolmate, John Howard, and is a reminder that the perils of the North Sea were not always those posed by nature.

AN encounter on the North Sea fishing grounds between a U-Boat and three Staithes fishing vessels in the summer of 1916 is described in a book by John Howard, the historian of the North Riding village. It ended with two of the fishermen's craft being sent to the bottom, but there was no loss of life, and the affair seems to have been conducted with courtesy on both sides.

Mr Howard gives July 13 1916 as the date of the incident, and names the U-Boat commander as Werner Fürbringer. This man, known to his comrades as "Fips", was then aged 29 and in his first command, UB-39. He sank a lot of ships during the First World War, and in 1933 wrote an account of his adventures, which eventually appeared in an English edition in 1999.

The day before his encounter with the Staithes men, he had audaciously gone close inshore and, surfacing at dusk, inflicted a bombardment on the County Durham town of Seaham. His target was a foundry where he supposed munitions were being made, and he loosed off a hundred 8.8-cm rounds from a deck-gun. None hit the target and there were suggestions later that this was a deliberate act of mercy, designed to spare the folk living in the streets clustered round the factory.

Werner Fürbringer, commander of the U-Boat UB-39.

It is a mark of the man that Fips' book had two dedications, one to a brother who fell at Verdun at the end of May 1916, and the other to Mrs Mary Slaughter, who, on the evening of May 12, was taking a country walk near Seaham when she was injured by a shell "fired by the German submarine UB-39, and succumbed to her terrible injuries at Sunderland Hospital the following morning, the only casualty of the incident".

He makes no specific reference to the Staithes encounter, but records that the day after the bombardment his submarine resumed the commerce war, and quickly sank 14 steam trawlers and a number of smaller craft. He recognised their crews as a special breed, ever ready to return to sea

William Francis Verrill,
1847 – 1935.

despite the dangers. Fips wrote: "I always treated them as well as I could when taking them aboard, and we often used to have chats, seaman to seaman".

This humanitarian attitude is amply borne out by Mr Howard. He identifies the Staithes boats as *Success, Mary Ann* and *Richard*. Their crews were taken aboard the U-Boat, and two were sunk, the exception being *Richard*, which was badly damaged and allowed to drift away. She survived, together with her catch of 5,000 herrings, and her owners recovered her from the Tees the following day.

Fürbringer was left with 11 survivors cluttering the deck of UB-39, and took the opportunity to send them safely home when he encountered a fourth Staithes vessel, George Cole's *Venus*. Before transferring his captives, Fips offered them a drink of water, apologising for a lack of tea or coffee.

George Cole, a Deacon of the Congregational Church, mistook the nature of the beverage and upbraided the U-Boat commander: "You've just sunk their bits o'cobles. Are you trying to corrupt 'em wi' strang drink an all?" Fips' response was a farewell: "Goodbye gentlemen. I have done with you now."

Among the victims of this episode was William Francis Verrill, whom Mr Howard describes as one of the most colourful personalities in Staithes, irascible, engaging, a formidable preacher, and a master of wit and repartee. Throughout, he addressed Oberleutnant Fürbringer as "Maister".

"Do you like herrings, Maister Francis (his brother)? chuck him a warp of herring ower." When the submarine closed up alongside his coble *Success*: "Fend off Maister. Ah deeant want mah bit o'coble screeaped. Ah've nobbut just had her pented." Verrill, known in Staithes as Billy Fanny, no doubt grieved when his coble was despatched to the bottom, but at least the incident added wonderfully to his stock of anecdotes.

Fips' destruction of the Staithes fishing boats may not feature in his memoirs, but at the time a German communiqué sought to legitimise the action by claiming the English fishermen were "keeping watch and doing intelligence work for the British Navy". In July 1918 Fips' new command, UB-111, was sunk off the northeast coast, and he was taken prisoner. He was held for a time in London for interrogation, and records being taken for exercise in Hyde Park where an old lady looked at his "gaunt, dogged, unshaved face" and gasped: "Oh, you're the most beast-like man I ever saw." She turned on her heel and wobbled off, and Fips noted she was broad of beam: "As I stared at her ample posterior, I knew that the U-Boat food blockage of England had failed."

Eventually, he was taken to a prisoner-of-war camp in Colsterdale, Yorkshire, where the inmates occupied huts originally built for Leeds Corporation waterworks' navvies and later used by the Leeds Pals Battalion while they were preparing for their obliteration on the Somme. Fips' navigation was amiss. He described Colsterdale as being "at Masham near Manchester".

He was repatriated in 1919, helped develop Hitler's Kriegsmarine, and was Senior Planning Officer, U-Boats, at the outbreak of the Second World War. He retired from the Kriegsmarine in 1943, and died in 1982, aged 91.

Fürbringer was rewarded for his gallantry in the Kaiser's War with the Iron Cross First and Second Class, and the Order of the House of Hohenzollern with Swords. He might also have taken pride in the fact that he was not held in dishonour by his foes, not even by those fishermen whose livelihoods he had destroyed.

* William Francis Verrill of Staithes and the German U-Boat *(£2.50) is available from the author, John Howard at 13 Tippy Butts, Scalby, Scarborough YO 13 0RF.* Fips, Legendary U-Boat Commander, *translated by Geoffrey Brookes (Leo Cooper, 1999).*

FROM BONFIRES TO BMEWS

FROM the time of the Roman watchtowers to the present-day Ballistic Missile Early Warning Station on the North York Moors, a careful watch has been kept from Yorkshire's shores for threats from abroad.

This surveillance naturally intensified when an attempt at invasion seemed likely, as happened during the reign of Queen Elizabeth I when the Armada sailed from Spain. A system of beacons was set up along the coast, able to communicate with each other and pass news inland of any suspicious sightings.

This was a development of an arrangement that had been in place since ancient times. The word beacon itself is Anglo-Saxon in origin, meaning a sign or token, and sharing its root with the term to beckon. From ancient times, the warning fires consisted of heaps of wood on promontories or high hills, but under King Edward III (1312-1377), the use of pitch was introduced.

The beacons then produced a good light by night, and plumes of black smoke by day, ensuring they could be seen over considerable distance. They were maintained at public expense by the levying of a rate called Beconagium, and the King was empowered, by Commission under his Great Seal, to cause them to be erected where considered necessary.

The system was reviewed with the utmost urgency under Elizabeth I when King Philip II of Spain threatened an invasion of her realm, and assembled a great fleet under the command of the Duke of Medina Sidonia. This Armada eventually sailed from Corunna in July 1588.

By then many anxious eyes scanned the horizon from England's shores. Orders disseminated by Royal Command called for a diligent watch to be kept, with this task going to the "wisest and discreetest" men available. A suggestion was added that none be allowed to watch "but honest householders, above the age of 30 years."

There were three beacons grouped together on sites near the coast, each containing a tar barrel, and with at least another barrel in reserve. One fire was to be lit if there was a suspicion that a passing ship was an enemy, two if a number aroused "vehement suspicion", and all three if the strange vessels were obviously enemies intent on landing.

The idea seized the imagination of the poet Lord Macaulay (1800-1859):

> *For swift to east and swift to west the ghastly war flame spread,*
> *High on St Michael's Mount it shone: it shone on Beachy Head.*
> *Far on the deep the Spaniard saw, along each southern shire,*
> *Cape beyond cape, in endless range, those twinkling points of fire.*

Beacon stations communicated with their neighbours, passing on any alarm. As Macaulay had it, "the red glare on Skiddaw roused the burghers of Carlisle". In the East Riding, Speeton "took light" from Flamborough, and "gave light" to Ruston on the Bridlington-Driffield Road. Then it was passed to Bishop Wilton, to Holme-on-Spalding Moor, and thence to York. Thus alerts spread almost literally like wildfire.

Although the beacons are long gone, their sites are commemorated by place-names like Beacon Field near Paull. Three fire baskets mounted on poles stood at a spot called "The Hooles" at Fylingdales. They could be seen from Barnby Beacon, located on the cliffs above Kettleness, and from Danby Beacon. Several sites, like Dimlington on the Holderness shore, have been washed away.

Small huts, built of turves, were sometimes provided for the watchers, and a Victorian Vicar of Mappleton, the Rev T. W. Kelly, was told by an elderly man that they were very comfortable, and he could remember one being occupied by a sentinel long after all the excitement had died away, and other people had settled back to ordinary life.

The Armada was defeated and its ships scattered to the winds. The next major threat was of invasion by Napoleon, but there were intermediate scares, the most notable of which emanated not from across the North Sea but the Atlantic. During the American War

John Paul Jones, who won a hard-fought battle off Flamborough Head in 1779.

of Independence, a Scottish-born adventurer, John Paul Jones (1747-92) took up arms on behalf of the Colonists, declaring an intention to "distress the enemies of the United States by sea or land".

He terrorised the west coast, landing at Whitehaven, capturing merchant ships, and even seizing a British warship, the *Drake*, 20 guns. Then in 1779, he sailed from Brest, France, in charge of a small squadron, and had the courage and effrontery to begin marauding in the North Sea. He had an early encounter with the homeward-bound Hull Baltic trader, *Crow Isle*, which somehow evaded his clutches, a feat which her owner, Francis Hall, celebrated by commissioning a dinner service from the Belle Vue Pottery in Hull. A plate that survives is illustrated by a scene from the merchantman's encounter with Jones, who was branded a pirate.

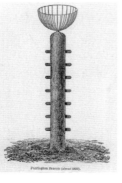

The 1889 edition of Old Yorkshire, *edited by William Smith, and published in London by Longmans, Green and Co, contained a contribution by J. Nicholson about Yorkshire Beacons which was illustrated by drawings, mostly made from memory, of beacon posts along the coast. These two examples from the book are of Hunsley Beacon in about 1830, drawn from a verbal description, and Patrington Beacon in about 1820.*

This ancient pile of weather-beaten chalk is sometimes called Flamborough Old Lighthouse, but it may never have served that function. It was put up in 1674 by Sir John Clayton, who made a business of building lighthouses, not entirely for altruistic reasons, for there was money to be made from tolls exacted from shipowners. However, it appears that the necessary funds were not forthcoming at Flamborough, and Sir John's fire remained unlit. The tower may have been used as a lookout and a beacon, of which there were at one time no fewer than three on the headland. One was near the southern end of Danes' Dyke, occupying a circular mound known as Beacon Hill. Another, at the north end of the Dyke, appeared on a map included in John Phillips' Geology of Yorkshire. *Sir John's tower may have been the third, for there is a recess at the top which could have served as a fireplace. (Mel Hulme/YPN)*

Such was his reputation that Speeton Beacon, and probably all the others from Scarborough to Flamborough Head, were lit when he appeared off the Yorkshire coast in September 1779, with four ships reputed to be armed with 124 guns, and near 1,100 men. Jones' intention was to prey on merchantmen in the Baltic trade, but after his sally at Whitehaven there were fears that he would land, and militiamen were drafted to the coast towns to resist him.

Jones, on his flagship *Bonne Homme Richard*, won a hard-fought battle off Flamborough Head against the frigate *Serapis*, 44 guns, and her small sister-ship, the *Countess of Scarborough*, 28 guns, Royal Navy vessels that were shepherding a fleet of 40 merchantmen on passage from the Baltic. Captain Richard Pearson of the *Serapis* eventually struck his flag after a battle that lasted three-and-a-half hours, but for Jones it was something of a Pyrrhic victory. The fight put up by the Royal Navy enabled the merchantmen to take shelter under the guns of Scarborough Castle, and *Bonne Homme Richard* was left a wreck, and sank the following day.

Capt Pearson does not seem to have been blamed for the loss of his ship. Grateful merchants rewarded him with a sword, and he was dubbed knight by the King. When Jones heard this, he is supposed to have said: "Should I have the good fortunate to fall in with him again, I'll make a lord of him".

The beacons fell into disuse during the 19th Century and most disappeared, but J. Nicholson of Hull compiled an account of *Beacons of East Yorkshire*. He also contributed to William Smith's *Old Yorkshire* in 1889, and illustrated his article with a number of drawings. These showed a variety of designs, and one included a view of a kind of hutment, presumably a shelter for watchers.

Coastguards maintain the seaward watch to this day, but during the First World War a system of early warning was put in place that relied on hearing instead of sight. A walk along the lane that winds up Boulby cliffs, near Staithes, brings into view a curious structure in pastureland. At first sight it seems as outlandishly mysterious as prehistoric standing stones, the Rudston Monolith, perhaps, or the Boroughbridge Arrows.

Its shape brings to mind a soccer goal facing the sea, with posts and nets cast in concrete. It is neither ancient nor beautiful, and has long outlived its usefulness. Yet it is protected, having been declared a Grade II listed building with star, a distinction owed to its rarity, history and intended function. What they have up there, at Boulby Barns, is a Sound Mirror hastily put into place after 1915, the year the Zeppelins came.

The idea was that its concave back would gather distant sounds of the Maybach engines that propelled the dirigibles through the air, and reflect them into a microphone. Amplified, the faraway rumble was transmitted to earphones worn by operators known as Listeners, who would then communicate a warning of impending air attack.

The Boulby Mirror stands not far from 666ft cliffs, where winds blow sharp as knives and raindrops fly like pellets. The Listeners had shelter of a sort in a trench, which was provided, not as a refuge but to prevent human obstruction of incoming airwaves. They must have spent hours huddled there, ears attuned for any sound different from the soughing of the wind and the crashing of the North Sea. Mostly they were Territorial Army volunteers trained by the Royal Engineers, but at some Mirrors blind men were also given a try, the idea being that their disability intensified their hearing.

This curious object is a Sound Mirror, made of rough-rendered slag concrete, which was set up near Redcar during the First World War and intended to give early warning of a Zeppelin attack on Middlesbrough.

They had an important task. The Skinningrove Ironworks, which occupied an exposed headland a short distance to the north, was a prime target for German raids. During the war it produced two-and-a-half- million tons of trinitrotoluene – TNT – used for filling shells for the Western Front. It was a horribly dangerous process, and for a time only two men were fully trained to oversee it, working round the clock in 12-hour shifts.

The official history of the Skinningrove Iron Company names one as C.F. Tidman, but curiously the other remains anonymous, being merely referred to as "a senior undergraduate from Birmingham University". The process was sufficiently hazardous for two components of the plant to be built on the edge of the cliff, so that in the event of an explosion, half the blast would be dissipated over the sea.

On the night of September 8th 1915, a Zeppelin commander called Odo Loewe, who had attacked Goole the previous month, killing 16 people, was back over Yorkshire, intent on destroying Skinningrove. He had difficulty in getting his bearings, and in desperation dropped his bombs where he thought the works might be.

Astonishingly, he achieved some hits. One bomb landed on the benzene house, but failed to penetrate the concrete roof. Another hit the TNT store, but did not explode. Aware of how close Loewe had been to sending a good part of the North Riding sky-wards, it is hardly surprising that the authorities sought early warning of further raids, and the Sound Mirror was placed at Boulby, a headland divided from Skinningrove by a deep ravine, in 1916.

The Mirrors may sound primitive, even a little absurd, but they functioned sufficiently well to impress the Royal Navy. When Zeppelins flew in support of an attempted raid on Sunderland by the German High Seas fleet in 1916, the British commander, Jellicoe, reported that "directional

Skinningrove Iron Works, perched on a headland to the north of Boulby Cliffs, was a tempting target for air attack in both World Wars, and in 1914-1918 received early warning from a Sound Mirror mounted at Boulby.

wireless stations" had identified at least 10 above the North Sea. The airships had a top speed of 60-80 mph, and could be detected by a Mirror at a distance of 20 miles, giving an invaluable quarter-of-an-hour to get Royal Flying Corps fighters into the air.

There was also time for an alert among the terraces of Skinningrove and the streets of the nearby town of Loftus. When an alarm was signalled, wardens went from door to door, hammering on them with wooden potato-mashers, giving householders time to take some kind of cover, under railway arches, maybe, or in air raid shelters like those at Loftus, which had been dug, perhaps insensitively, adjoining the town graveyard.

A mass attack by eight Zeppelins was mounted in May 1916. The leader, L23, dropped an incendiary bomb on Danby Moor, setting it ablaze. Some 25 minutes later, along came L16, and Werner Petersen, its commander, may well have bagged a few grouse out of season by dumping his entire bomb load on what he thought must be the target. A fourth Zeppelin, L17, did attack Skinningrove, and "a coastal city to the east", maybe Saltburn.

Other attempts were made to destroy Skinningrove Iron Works, and its official history reckons 100 bombs were aimed at it during 1914-18. Incendiaries dropped on the naphthalene pans, which must have been worrying, and high explosive bombs plunged into slag heaps. The only damage was to the steel plant offices.

Faith in Sound Mirrors persisted between the wars, and the biggest of all, a 200ft arc of concrete, was erected on the Kent coast in 1928.

But between 1939 and 1945, when the Yorkshire coast was again threatened by German raiders, there was no longer any need to post Listeners at the strange concrete "ears". On moorland above Danby had risen the 360ft lattice towers of a radar station, which came into operation on Good Friday, 1939, and had a direct telephone line to RAF Fighter Command headquarters.

The site it occupied, nearly 1,000ft above sea level, is named Beacon Hill, recalling alerts of an earlier age.

'BONNIE GEORDIE' AND THE AWFUL STINK

IN the summer of 1876, a small flotilla was greeted on arrival in Whitby harbour by cannon booming out a salute, martial airs played by the band of the Volunteer Artillery Corps, a flutter of bunting, and hearty cheers from hundreds of people gathered on the quays and piers.

As the *Whitby Times* commented, it was as if the Royal Yacht or the Channel Fleet was making port under a press of canvas.

Yet the vessels accorded so tumultuous a greeting were a steam tugboat towing a dredger called the *Mole*, with three hoppers bobbing along in the rear.

The populace had good cause for rejoicing. At last something was to be done about Whitby's Awful Stink, caused by an accumulation of filth in the harbour. The *Mole*, watched by enthralled crowds, began her work above the bridge where conditions, again according to the *Whitby Times*, had "long been in a deplorable state, and most offensive to the public."

The trouble was that Whitby had no sewage system and everything – literally everything – went into the harbour. Nor was there much prospect of the problem being solved, the ratepayers having shied away in alarm from an engineer's recommendation that they should spend £40,000 to pipe effluent to sea.

Enter then the hero of this story, Sir George Elliot MP, who had become the first leader of the nation's coal industry to receive a baronetcy in 1874. He had a substantial interest in Whitby, having acquired the West Cliff Estate, formerly owned by George Hudson, "The Railway King". Following Hudson's financial collapse, the Royal Hotel and boarding houses he had built on the West Cliff passed to the North Eastern Railway Company, until Sir George extricated the estate "from the jaws of Chancery", according to a contemporary account.

Sir George had begun his working life as a boy at the Pensher Colliery in the Durham coalfield, owned by the Marquess of Londonderry. At 17 he was apprenticed to a land surveyor, and his progress was such that in his forties he acquired the pit where he had started work. He became a major shareholder and general manager of the Powell Duffryn Steam Coal Company in Wales. He was a partner in the firm that laid the first trans-Atlantic cable and carried out port works at Newport, Monmouthshire, and Alexandria in Egypt. He was President of the Institute of Mining Engineers (1868-69) and a MP for three different constituencies over the period 1868-1892.

This great industrialist, known in the coalfield as "Bonnie Geordie", and backed by enormous wealth (he left £561,044 when he died in December 1893) took on something almost as formidable as the Awful Stink, the Wonderful Inertia displayed by Whitby's Pier and Harbour Trustees.

He wanted to ensure the success of his investment in the town by attracting holidaymakers to the West Cliff. To that end he built the Saloon (now the nucleus of the Whitby Spa complex), and laid out pleasure grounds. He realised that the state of the harbour was a powerful deterrent to visitors, and engaged an engineer called Abernethy to produce a plan setting out possible improvements and their estimated cost.

Sir George soon found that it is one thing to have grand plans for Whitby, but quite another to have them implemented. What he had done, sadly, was fail to learn the lesson of history. In 1864, the North Eastern Railway Company called a meeting of Whitby's good and great at the Royal Hotel and laid before them a vision of what might be achieved for the town "if only those immovable local authorities would afford the needful co-operation". Lamented the *Whitby Gazette*: "This golden opportunity passed away."

Eventually, in a bid to get things moving, Sir George said that, if the necessary rights, powers and interests were made over to him, he would guarantee to make the harbour safe and commodious for fishing craft, and for refuge and shelter. The *Whitby Times* in its obituary of Sir George commented that "this public-spirited and liberal overture was not met in a friendly spirit." In short, it was turned down flat.

Where the Harbour Trustees were prepared to meet Sir George was in the matter of the dredger, for even the local worthies acknowledged that the "offensive smell" emanating from the harbour was an unmitigated nuisance, especially at low tide. So Sir George arranged with his fellow River Wear Commissioners for the loan of a dredger, hoppers and steam-tug to clear the noxious accumulations from the harbour bed.

He suggested the Trustees might go halves with the cost, but they replied they had no funds for dredging. However they assured Sir George they would "cordially sanction the experimenting with a dredger for one month at his own cost."

So it was that in that summer of 1876, as the Awful Stink wafted over the town, the dredger *Mole* and her attendant vessels were given a resounding greeting, and watched as they went about their work by great and appreciative multitudes, presumably with handkerchiefs to their noses. The dredging went on until December, and 21,356 tons of spoil were shipped to sea.

Sir George continued his links with Whitby, and stayed at the Royal Hotel at the end of the 1892 season. He had, however, never completed Hudson's plans for the West Cliff, leaving Royal Crescent half-finished and abandoning further development towards Upgang. It seems his initial enthusiasm had waned after such setbacks as the rebuff administered to his harbour scheme. Also, some years before his death he signalled lack of interest by handing over the West Cliff Estate to his son George, who succeeded him to the baronetcy.

Sir George's later years were clouded by the loss of his Monmouth Boroughs parliamentary seat in the 1892 general election This came two years after being sued for breach of promise of marriage by a professional singer, Emiline Hairs. She claimed £5,000, which he could easily have afforded if he had wished to avoid publicity, but he chose instead to fight the action in the Queen's Bench Division, and engaged Sir Charles Russell QC to state his case.

A Mr Kemp QC, representing Miss Hairs, referred to Sir George's pursuit of her and declared that "there was no fool like an old fool", whereupon Sir George himself piped up from the well of the court, "Hear, hear". He won the action, though.

• *Eventually, Whitby got a sewerage scheme with an outflow on the Scaur to the Saltwick side of the East Pier that was exposed at low tide. Yorkshire Water has now replaced this with a treatment plant and ancillary works costing £32m.*

WHITBY, FROM LIGHTHOUSE. 6990. G.W.W.

Constant dredging has ensured a vast improvement in the depth of water in Whitby harbour since Sir George Elliot's day. This shows a bucket dredger at work. She is probably the predecessor of the Esk dredger, aquired by Whitby between the wars.

THEN AND NOW – WHITBY

A view of Whitby beach dating from the days before the extensions were added to the pier. There is perhaps an air of expectancy. The bathing machines have been positioned near the water, the donkeys wait patiently, the deck chairs have been set up, but where are the people? Perhaps the picture was taken early in the morning before the day had got into full swing....

.... ah, that's more like it. Here is a photograph of a crowded beach, with curious little circular tents in the foreground, and an array of bathing machines to the left.

Whitby Abbey is visible on the skyline as Endeavour *proceeds in triumph up the town's harbour. Cheered on by huge crowds, she heads for a berth not a stone's throw from the site of Thomas Fishburn's yard, where Captain Cook's original ship, a cat-built baroque intended for the coal trade, was built. The 1997 visit of this replica, constructed in Fremantle, Western Australia, attracted visitors in unprecedented numbers and transformed Whitby's fortunes. (Gerard Binks/YPN)*

An unusual view of Whitby is a rarity, but here is a clever one, looking across from the vicinity of the 199 steps to what was once known as Boots' Corner. The cluster of roofs, mostly of red pantiles, is dominated by the clock tower atop the Town Hall erected by Nathaniel Cholmley in 1788. It was at a meeting here in 1823 that a group of Whitby worthies, members of the town's newly-formed Literary and Philosophical Society, agreed to find rooms to exhibit a collection of curiosities. From that decision sprang the Society's Pannett Park Museum, one of Whitby's great but relatively unsung wonders.

The freelance photographer Alan Wastell took this shot for the Whitby Gazette *in March 2006. It is surely one of the news pictures of the year, and shows traffic apparently proceeding normally while a tremendous sea bursts on the wall at Sandsend, flinging water above the height of buildings across the front.*

Alan Wastell was also on hand when a wave erupted heaven-wards near Whitby's West Pier slipway in March 2006 The picture brings to mind Frank Meadow Sutcliffe's familiar shot of a wave steepling up White West Pier lighthouse. The sea rarely reaches that height, but a repetition of Sutcliffe's wave was witnessed by my cousin Bryan Barker (former headmaster of Whitby School, now Whitby Community College) in early 2007. He saw a surge engulf the extensions, then leap as high as the lighthouse, which stands 75ft tall.

BAY BEFORE
THE HOLIDAY-COTTAGERS
– MR PENNOCK'S MEMORIES

Richard Beene Pennock left a wonderful legacy for Robin Hood's Bay, where he was born and lived all his life. He made tape recordings of his memories of the village, its people and their customs for the Fylingdales Local History Society, and also wrote them down. Eventually they appeared as a book, *Robin Hood's Bay As I Have Known It,* **published by Cordelia Stamp under her Caedmon of Whitby imprint in 2002. A copy came my way, and this chapter is based on a review which appeared in the Yorkshire Post on 20th June, 2002.**

ROBIN HOOD'S BAY off-season is a pretty doleful place, especially when the clouds close in and a sharp wind rattles the pantiles. Streets and alleyways are deserted and the jostling cottages, most of which have been snapped up as holiday homes to the exclusion of locals, are empty.

It seems bereft of life, and the idea springs to mind that it might have been a kindness to put it out of its misery and let it all tumble into the North Sea, thus following a whole street on High Cliff, a row of cottages on the seaward side of King Street, and the back room of Florrie Sketton's cottage which, in 1947, fell down the cliff while she was having a nice cup of tea in the front parlour. Bay's seasonal soulless existence was brought about quickly, abruptly even. A lifetime sufficed, albeit a long one in the case of Richard Beene Pennock, for he saw most of the 20th Century, dying aged 93 in 1998. The manuscript, on which he had worked since his mid-80s, was among his belongings, and has been published posthumously, with the co-operation of his son, Raymond Pennock.

Here is a tale worthy of Jonathan Swift, for the Robin Hood's Bay of RB Pennock's early years is as strange and foreign to modern eyes as any imaginary Lilliput or Brobdignag visited by Gulliver on his travels. Mr Pennock was born down-Bank, in a cottage on Tyson's Row rented for £5 a year. Water came by the bucketful from a communal tap at the top of Tyson's Steps, and the weekly wash was humped to drying grounds where families paid the Lord of the Manor a shilling (5p) a year for use of the posts and lines.

There were no drains, and waste went over the cliff edge in chutes, or into middins. Mr Pennock, despite his manifest devotion to old days and ways, conceded that this was "unhygienic". His mother was a Storm, a member of the family on which Leo Walmsley based the Fosdykes in *Three Fevers*. His father was the eldest of 14 children, and like many Bay menfolk went to sea as soon as he was able. It was a perilous calling, and in 1909 he was swept from the deck of a steamship in the North Sea and never seen again. Subsequently, two of his brothers drowned, one in Montevideo Bay, and the other with an entire crew when a U-Boat sank their merchantman in 1917. Another of Mr Pennock's uncles, this time on his mother's side, was lost in the Humber while

Traditional fishing villages, clustered between the North Sea and steep cliffs, are a special feature of the Yorkshire coast. Robin Hood's Bay is barely visible from Bank Top, where this picture is taken, for its picturesque huddle of cottages, shops, inns and alleyways lies deep in a cleft in the cliffs. On the horizon is Ravenscar, the site intended by Victorian entrepreneurs as another railway resort.
(Mel Hulme/YPN)

The characteristic features of Robin Hood's Bay are also seen at Staithes, which of necessity had to grow upwards rather than sideways, as demonstrated by this photograph showing three or four-storey buildings. An article in the Leeds Mercury Weekly Supplement, *reprinted in* Old Yorkshire *(1889), contained the warning: "Streets there are none. Every path is painfully crooked and ill-paved, and for a stranger to descend through the village after nightfall is difficult and even dangerous." The same writer categorised Staithes folk as strong and bony, "speaking an unmusical accent". (Simon Hulme/YPN)*

an apprentice on the Whitby-owned *SS Hawsker*.

In these circumstances, his mother understandably preferred Richard Pennock safe on dry land, and for a time he worked as a counter-hand up the Bank at Top-Shop, owned by R.K. Storm. He then joined the shop and bakery down-Bank at Bridge End, known for many years as Haslops', and worked there until the early 1960s, when Keith Hamlin acquired the business.

In his early days, it was the practice of householders to take their bread and mid-day meals to the bakery to be cooked. On Sundays, they would arrive with their meat and potatoes at 10.30 am and return with Yorkshire puddings at 11.15 am. Cakes, too, were baked, and one woman just sent homemade mincemeat, as she preferred Haslops' pastry casings to her own. Gingerbread and hot cross buns were the bakery's specialities, although the latter were not a year-round delicacy, and never ever produced before Good Friday. Then, beginning at 4 am, 1,000 were made before noon, and sold at a penny each.

Robin Hood's Bay was largely self-supporting. Most folk had sidelines. Neddy Peacock specialised in boots and shoes, but also offered mint, gooseberries and rhubarb from his allotment. Jack Wedgewood, the plumber and electrician, built his own fishing boat. Edwin Collinson kept the Bay Hotel and was the Parish rate collector. Ned Readman at the Dolphin was the village road-sweeper. Jack Russell from Linger's Farm delivered milk from cans hanging from a yoke. It came in pennorths or ha'pennorths, and there was always "a drop for t'cat". Jack preferred something stronger, and while in the Laurel he would leave his cans in the street with the message, "help y'sen". He was reputed to have had an encounter with the Linger's End ghost, perhaps after one of those halts at the Laurel.

John Duck ran a carrier's business, and would go down-Bank blowing a whistle to signal his arrival. He was given messages to take, asked to buy this and that from Whitby shops, and entrusted with parcels to deliver, and off he would go on his horse and cart, returning later in the day with various missions accomplished. A retired master mariner, Thomas Cooper, provided the village with its own buses, Heather Motor Services, running to and from Whitby.

People knew their places, and were kept in them firmly. The Vicar, the Rev Jermyn Cooper, expected a curtsey form the village girls and looked to the boys to doff their caps. Master mariners provided a kind of local aristocracy, and Mr Pennock reckoned that as many as 60 sea captains lived in Bay, most of them up-Bank, where they placed figure-heads in their gardens, and gave their villas the names of their ships, Roma, Orb, Stanton, Aurora, Corra Lyn, Rokeby and Trongate to list but a few.

There was room for characters, too. Thomas Henry Booth's names were unknown until he died. Everybody called him Ben the Barber, for he cut hair, and went from door to door selling matches, boot-laces, and small packets of baking powder. He lived behind shuttered windows and a locked door, and neighbours, taking pity on him, gave him eggs, tea and sugar and other comestibles. When he died, his cottage contained quantities of these gifts, stored away in cupboards, and in an advanced state of decomposition. In addition, hundreds of three-penny bits and other coins were found stuffed into matchboxes.

Thomas Dixon, the village carpenter, left a legacy in many houses of floors, skirtings and other fittings, beautifully and simply crafted from pitch pine His hobby was violin-making, and he created 38 instruments in the style of various masters like Stradivarius and Amati. These he polished to a gloss resembling a newly-peeled horse chestnut. He also built two pianos, making the keys from the bones that came with Sunday joints of meat, and an organ with pipes fashioned from Lyle's Golden Syrup tins. He was, perhaps, a genius, and now has a memorial in print, thanks to Richard Pennock, whose book will make instructive reading for those visiting Bay in the 21st Century. It brings into fine focus the time not so very long ago when it was a community, populous, proud, self-sufficient, busy, vital, in short, very much alive.

On revisiting Robin Hood's Bay shortly before his death, Leo Walmsley remarked on how little it had changed. These two pictures make the same point. One was taken in June 1949 and the other in August 1964. They are remarkably alike despite the lapse of 15 years, apart from the sea wall that is part of Bay's protection against erosion. It could even be the same ice-cream van.

THE MAN WITH NO SOCKS

Leo Walmsley must have a place in a book about the Yorkshire coast, for he was its most able chronicler, especially in his novel *Three Fevers*, one of the great books of the 20th Century.

LEO Walmsley was held in some awe in our family. He was supposed to have borrowed money from Grandfather Barker, who was editor of the *Whitby Gazette*. This was a rare feat, for Grandfather was reputed to be canny with his brass, and was decorated for encouraging thrift, being appointed MBE for his services to the National Savings movement.

Although it is recalled with admiration by the Barkers, Walmsley probably forgot this transaction, although it is recalled with admiration by the Barkers. He was a man much troubled by penury, and unlikely to recall a single creditor.

Until towards its end, Walmsley's was a rackety life, as emerges from his biography *Shells and Bright Stones* (Smith Settle, 2001), which Nona Stead produced by combining her own writing with that of four fellow-members of the Walmsley Society, Walmsley's widow Stephanie, and two of his five children.

He seems to have had a weird looking-glass existence, where nothing was exactly what it seemed. Far from being an only child, as he liked to present himself, he had three brothers and a sister, who Lionel – Leo - seems to have somehow excised from his life.

He was married to Joe, Helen, Billy, Claire, Wendy and Suzanne, and so far we have only reached his first wife, for that is the catalogue of names he used for her. Her real name was not even on the list, for she was christened Elsie Susanna Preston, but she chose to be Suzanne, much as Lionel opted for Leo. Theirs was a love-match. Even though they had already separated when his only major best-seller, *Three Fevers*, was published, she was the girl in the dedication: "To Suzanne in the wind of a Bramblewick Spring".

They had no children, and in a letter to her former husband written twelve years after their divorce, Suzanne attributed their marriage breakdown to India rubber, presumably a reference to their exercise of birth control.

No such precautions seem to have been taken second time around, and he and Margaret Bell-Little had four children. To an extent, Suzanne suffered the fate of Leo's brothers and sister. Although he kept in touch with her, he did not like to talk about his time with her, and so far as his two subsequent wives were concerned, she might never have existed.

Yet Helen or Claire or Suzanne or whoever seems to have been pivotal to his life. They married in 1919. Leo Walmsley was a handsome young airman with the Military Cross, awarded for gallantry over Africa in 1917. He had shed his Yorkshire accent (another disappearing trick) and was building a reputation as a writer, with magazine articles published, and a book, *Flying and Sport in East Africa* (Blackwood, 1920) in preparation.

He needed to apply himself at that crucial stage in his life, and get his nose to the grindstone of creative writing, a painful and wearing process that has trimmed the aspirations of many a writer. Encouragement to do so was not forthcoming from his captivating young bride. She tirelessly sought the company of painters, sculptors, and others she regarded as intellectuals, and relished a round of parties, receptions and sunlit holidays. She preferred Italy to the North Riding of Yorkshire, and it is strikingly appropriate that when the break-up did come, Suzanne made off to Florence with the sculptor Barbara Hepworth, while Leo Walmsley returned to Robin Hood's Bay.

For years, in a literary sense, he seems to have lost his way, and it was 1932 before Cape brought out *Three Fevers* to public acclaim, and praise from such notable figures as J.B. Priestley ("grandly alive") and Rebecca West ("a perfect word-spinner"). His financial worries eased. National British Films paid him £300 in advance of his five-per-cent of the profits of the film of the book, *Turn of the Tide*. Alas, it was not a box-office hit, and failed to recoup more than a third of the production cost of £30,000 put up by another Yorkshireman, J Arthur Rank, whose first film it was.

Years later, Barrie Farnill, a colleague of mine on the *Yorkshire Evening Post*, asked Walmsley why he had left Bay in the first place. The reply was: "I owed money." *Three Fevers* enabled him to settle with his more pressing creditors, and encourage his return to Robin Hood's Bay with Margaret Bell-Little, whom he had married in 1933, soon after his divorce from Suzanne had been made absolute.

In 1935 he and Margaret set up home in a converted barn and beasthouse at Leith Rigg above Fylingdales, and remained there until 1941. Their finances improved when the third Bramblewick novel, *Sally Lunn*, appeared in 1937, and quickly ran through five impressions.

Three Fevers centres on two fishing families, the Fosdykes (Storms) and the Lunns (Dukes). Walmsley's sympathies were with the Dukes, but how deeply he penetrated that close-knit family is unclear. Richard Duke (Steve Lunn) recalled later that Walmsley did not fish regularly in their coble but spent a lot of time hanging round the family – "and never ever wore socks".

No doubt he developed a deep and lasting respect for the Dukes. They conferred on him their knowledge of the sea; he granted them a form of immortality, for they feature in all his Bramblewick novels, of which by far the best and most likely to last is *Three Fevers*.

Taken together, these books bear out the idea that Walmsley was not so much a creative writer as a highly skilled reporter, who could draw on his experience and acquired knowledge to weave the most wondrous and beguiling patterns of words.

His relationship with the fisherfolk was not the straightforward comradeship it seemed. He wrote to a friend, Dr Sam Wilson: "I'm all out for the alleged lower class against the middle-class, because I think a man like Henry Duke is worth any two of us". Thus, for all his begging and scrounging, the barefoot writer saw himself as occupying a superior station in the class structure to that of the hard-working fisherfolk who provided his raw material.

Unlike them, he was "one of us", and the suspicion arises that he observed them in much the same way as he examined sea creatures washed into rock pools on the Scaur. Bay folk may have sniffed this out. Many detested Leo Walmsley. Apart from his lack of what they would regard as a proper job, he offended an essentially Christian community by setting up home with Margaret Bell-Little while still married to Suzanne.

His third wife, Stephanie, was herself the daughter of a gifted writer and newspaper columnist Nat Gubbins. She recalled that her husband had disciplined himself into writing, and spent four hours each day at his typewriter. They shared an idyll at Fowey, Cornwall, but Walmsley would hark back to his childhood: "Wait till you see my Bay", he would tell Stephanie, "It will knock spots off anything you have seen before". In 1963 he published *Paradise Creek* (Collins), another autobiographical work concerning his efforts to win back Margaret Bell-Little, from whom he was divorced in 1955, and their children, his home by the creek in Cornwall, and eventual meeting and happiness with Stephanie.

In 1965, he returned briefly to Robin Hood's Bay, having been commissioned by the *Yorkshire Post* to write on "Bay past and present". After a few days he returned to Leeds, where he told Barrie Farnill: "It was the most extraordinary experience of my whole life." The weather, a golden October week, had been like summer. He had revelled in the lonely beaches, and one day had stripped and bathed off Boggle Hole. The water had been warmer than in Fowey harbour, he claimed. He had been greeted by many friends of his youth, including Mabel Wedgewood, the village postman's daughter, who played the piano for local dances. The article he produced spoke of his joy that the village was unchanged and changeless.

He told Barrie: "I want to bring Stephanie here when the primroses are in bloom." A holiday flat was arranged for Leo and Stephanie and their daughter Selina for the following spring. A TV documentary was being planned, with him as writer and narrator. But it was not to be. Before any of the plans could be realised, Leo Walmsley was struck down by a fatal illness, and died in 1966. As he wished, his ashes were scattered in the sea.

THE ROYAL MYTH OF RAVENSCAR

ONE of the most persistent Yorkshire myths concerns His Majesty King George III, and his supposed incarceration at Ravenscar, near Robin Hood's Bay. This notion gets a frequent airing in magazines and newspapers, and has also achieved credence in books and coastal guides. In 1993 Adam Hart-Davis mentioned it in one of his television programmes.

The King, who succeeded in 1760, reigned until his death on 29th January 1820, by which time the madness that had closed in periodically during his long life had totally overwhelmed him. For his last nine years on the throne his son, who succeeded as George IV, acted as Prince Regent.

Known affectionately to his subjects as "Farmer George", the monarch is supposed to have been brought to Yorkshire to recuperate far from the public eye at Raven Hall, which, greatly extended and altered, became in the 19th Century what it is today, a fine hotel commanding wonderful views.

The headland on which it is perched, once the site of a Roman signal station, is one of the windiest spots in Yorkshire and is beyond argument thoroughly bracing. Two centuries ago, though, and throughout the reign of George III, it had a noisome neighbour, the Peak alum works, which first went into production in 1615. Not far away was a similar enterprise at Stoupe Brow.

'The Victorian Raven Hall, from an old photograph'

Raven Hall as it was in the days of William Henry Hammond.

The process of extracting alum from vast quarries that still scar the cliffs made the works unpleasant neighbours. Smoke and fumes belched day and night from the huge clamps, as much as 150ft across and 200ft high, in which the newly-won rock was burned at the start of the extraction process. More smoke came from furnaces, which at Peak in the 1820s were reckoned to consume 3,600 tons of coal every year. This mingled with the steam rising from lead or copper pans measuring some 45 feet square, where liquor extracted from the calcined rock was boiled until the alum crystallised . Also, there was the rancid stink from great quantities of urine and kelp, which were added as part of the brew.

With all this going on below, a vantage point from the grounds of Raven Hall, which offers so delightful a prospect today, must then have resembled standing in an anteroom of hell. A visitor spoke of sulphurous fumes stopping the breath, "a pestiferous effluvium", and wondered how any creature could live and work in such an atmosphere.

The possibility of Raven Hall, or Peak Hall as it was then known, being considered a suitable place of convalescence for anyone, let alone a deranged monarch, seems extremely unlikely. The mansion was built in about 1774, on the site of an older dwelling, for Captain William Child of the First, or King's, Regiment of Light Dragoons, who may have been posted to Yorkshire to help revenue men in their attempts to curb smuggling. Child, apparently a wealthy man, also had a financial interest in the production of alum, so perhaps for him the odours prevailing near his new abode could be borne quite equably in the expectation of profit.

Alum was, in fact, a source of wealth for many. It was a chemical compound that fixed dyes in cloth, and was used in the preparation of leather, paper, medicine and even cosmetics. David Pybus and John Rushton, in their contribution to a series of lectures brought together by David B Lewis in 1991 as *The Yorkshire Coast* (Normandy Press), reported suggestions that it was used to loosen teeth, and whiten cheap bread sold to the poor. They reckoned the annual demand at the time of Queen Elizabeth I as 1,000 tons a year, and in Georgian times it was a major British industry.

A great deal of rock was need to produce a small quantity of alum, yet George Young, the Whitby historian, recorded that during the years 1805-1817 the Peak and Stoupe Brow works were shipping out 300 tons a year between them. Stoupe Brow ceased production in 1817, but Peak continued until the 1860s.

On Capt Child's death, the estate passed to his daughter Ann, who was married to one of the sons of Francis Willis, a physician with a reputation for success in treating mental derangement. He first attended George III in 1788, and had a house at Greatford, Lincolnshire, which he used as a retreat for his patients, and later added another at nearby Shillingthorpe. Three of Willis's sons also took up medicine, and attended George III, being, like their father, early exponents of a quackish form of psychiatry.

However, the son who married Ann Child, Richard Willis, followed a different career path and joined the Royal Navy. He was an admiral when he died in 1829. His widow died shortly afterwards, and in about 1831 their son, the Rev Richard Child Willis, who had followed his grandfather and uncles into medicine as well as taking Holy Orders, inherited Raven Hall.

No doubt the stories about George III being incarcerated at the hall derive from the Willis ownership, but the dates are wrong. A Scarborough Archaeological and Historical Society

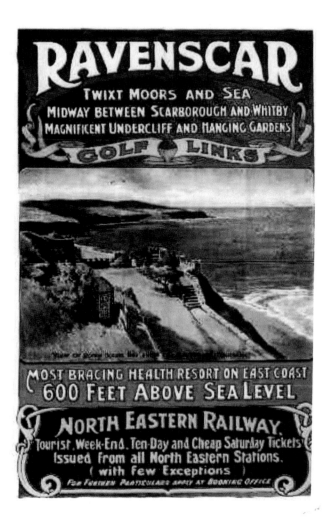

Ravenscar might have joined Saltburn, Hornsea and Withernsea as a railway resort, but few of the building plots laid out on the headland were developed. The North Eastern Railway Company was undoubtedly justified in claiming it to be the "most bracing health resort on the East coast" – just too bracing perhaps for some people.

publication, *The History of Ravenscar and Staintondale* (1988), asserts that Ravenscar had no direct connection with George III and, given the evidence (or lack of it), that seems beyond debate.

The Society, however, conceded that for decades the headland was awash with rumours, one of the most scurrilous and unseemly being that the Rev Richard Child Willis was an illegitimate son of the monarch, fathered by George III on one of the unmarried royal princesses. Certainly, the Squarson's behaviour was occasionally eccentric, perhaps sufficiently so to conjure the idea of madness among his forbears. He extended and renovated the mansion, celebrating the completion of the refurbishment by treating all 90 workmen to what he called a "sumptuous dinner" (known locally as a Rearing Supper and recalled over many years to come with awe and wonder). Stables were laid out with straw where guests who became incapable could be deposited, and a servant was detailed to observe whether they were alive or dead.

Richard Child Willis laid out the cliff terraces, built battlements, and, having failed to persuade trees to grow, put up cast-iron replicas instead, complete with metal leaves that tinkled pleasingly in the wind.

Invited to preach at St Mary's Parish Church in Whitby, he astonished the congregation by stripping off his coat and vest before ascending the three-decker pulpit. He was a notorious gambler, and lost heavily at Doncaster Races. He did not restrict his bets to horses either, and would stake guineas on which of two wood-lice would be first across a saucer.

His estate was mortgaged, and when he could not keep up the payments the mortgagee foreclosed, and William Henry Hammond, an auctioneer and land agent of Chancery Lane and Bell Yard, London, took possession of the hall and grounds in 1841. He proved a benevolent squire, and on his death in 1885 a Scarborough newspaper recorded that he created farmland out of wild moorland, and "changed heather into turnips, corn and pasture". He built a church, "open to the services of all Christians, conforming or otherwise", a manse for the minister, a mill, an inn, a shop, cottages and homesteads. Also, he was the moving force behind that wonderful scenic railway linking Scarborough with Whitby that opened in the year of his death. "His perseverance", recorded the *Whitby Gazette*, was "literally indomitable".

His great-grandson, Christopher Fry, the playwright, who died in 2005 aged 97, wrote a memoir, *Can You Find Me* (Oxford University Press, 1978) in which he referred to Raven Hall as a place of magic and history, a summer playground for his great-grandfather's nine children and 36 grandchildren, who were invited in relays.

Fry recalled that the hall was sold out of the family 12 years before he was born, but on visits he had seen the windows reflecting the sun and storms over the North Sea. He added: "In my early thoughts the hall was one with the Taj Mahal and the Acropolis, something then unvisited but revered, a monument to the expansive summer days when God looked benevolently on the family".

Later, a development company had the extraordinary idea of creating a holiday resort on the headland, where even the thickest hedges bow in obeisance to the wind, and that seems to have been when the name Ravenscar was coined. The notion was crazy enough to have emanated from Richard Child Willis. Perhaps mischievously, he had left in the grounds of the hall an object that helped keep the rumour-mill grinding, a royal coat-of-arms carved in stone. Sadly for the mythmakers, students of heraldry have pointed out that a Hanoverian escutcheon is missing, and it is in the style adopted in the reign of Queen Victoria.

Thus any idea that it is evidence of a Royal stay is an insubstantial as the sea-frets that sometimes shroud the headland. George III's incarceration makes a good story, but, alas, it is quite spoiled by the facts.

SIR GEORGE'S RIVER

IN early March 1999, first snow and then heavy rain swept the North York Moors. Rain gauges showed unprecedented readings, 10 inches in 12 days at Farndale and similar figures elsewhere. It was the kind of downpour expected perhaps once in a thousand years, and the rivers draining the uplands were soon in flood.

The Rye was so high that it was off the clock, having topped its gauge. The Seven reached an awesome 10ft deep thrice in five days. Pickering Beck ran four ft above normal. Unsurprisingly, Malton was flooded as it had been in 1930, 1931, 1947, 1960, 1963, and 1981. But this was the worst flood of all, worse even than the great inundation of 1931. With the Derwent up to 14ft 4ins above normal, this was hardly surprising.

But it could have been worse, much worse.

While the smaller streams and rivers flowing from the moorland were bursting their banks, the upper Derwent debouched from Forge Valley at about its normal level throughout those desperate days. Its upper reaches did not escape the downpour. Torrents spilled down such feeder streams as Jugger Howe Beck and Woof Howe Grain, Helwath Beck and Cowgate Slack.

But near Scalby, the water that might have turned flooding downstream from a disaster into a catastrophe was turned aside. Instead of running down Forge Valley into the Vale of Pickering, it cascaded into the North Sea near Scalby Mills. The Derwent's man-made safety valve had saved the day.

In flat meadows near Hackness the fury of the flood turned aside from the river and entered a waterway created in the first decade of the 19th Century, known as the Sea Cut.

In fine weather, this is little more than a stream ambling its way to the North Sea by way of Scalby Beck, and its flow at such times, was reckoned by the old Yorkshire Ouse and Hull River Authority at little more than 3,000,000 gallons a day. But let the storm clouds empty over the moors, or the snowdrifts melt in a rapid thaw, and the Cut is transformed. It surges high between its banks, its waters crashing over weirs "designed to abate scouring of the bed", with a deafening roar. The River Authority then gauged its flow at up to 540,000,000 gallons a day

The waterway was the inspiration of the inventive baronet Sir George Cayley (1771-1857), an engineer and pioneer of aviation. He lived at Brompton, on the road from Scarborough to Thornton-le-Dale, and had first-hand experience of the vagaries of the Derwent. He led a group of landowners who realised that unless the river could be brought under some kind of control, there would be no end to the recurrent floods in the low-lying Vale of Pickering.

The problem was a legacy of the Ice Age. As ice lay along the coast, the river was unable to follow its old course direct into the sea. Instead it turned inland, and meandered away from the coast, through Kirkham Gorge, and across Yorkshire to reach the sea via the Humber.

The response of Sir George and his supporters to this act of nature was an Act of Parliament, the Muston and Yedingham Drainage Act of 1800. This granted powers to open the Sea Cut because

*Scalby Mill has long been a favoured destination for visitors to
Scarborough. Theakston's Guide (1860) recommended its "refreshing
luxury of tea and cakes", which had acquired celebrity "from their
general excellence". It is also the place where water diverted from the
Derwent by the Sea Cut reaches the sea.*

natural waterways were "very insufficient to contain and convey the floodwaters".

Some 40 years ago I visited the Cut and met Alfred Fendley, who had been foreman in charge
for 30 years, and still lived in a small stone cottage where the waterway linked with the Derwent.
He recalled a drought in 1929 when the Cut dried out. Soon afterwards came heavy rain, and the
Cut ran so deep that it brimmed over, flooding some bungalows.

Subsequently, it was widened, its banks were heightened, and its weirs made good. The
waterway falls 100ft in its short journey from the Derwent to the sea. This was quite a contrast for
Mr Fendley, who had once worked on a river in Norfolk that fell only 3ft 9ins in 15 miles.

The Cut begins at Mowthorp between Hackness and Forge Valley, and joins Scalby Beck, a
busy stream that once powered four water mills, to complete its journey to the sea. In doing so,
geologists believe that it is more or less on the course followed by the Derwent before the
intervention of the Ice Age.

THEN AND NOW – SCARBOROUGH

Quayside scene in September 1959.

A safety boat on the beach at North Bay in June 1951.

Scarborough was basking in sunshine on the last day of May in 1966, and there was little room for sand-castle building on the beach.

Opposite. Cuthbert Brodrick's Grand Hotel dominates – nay, crushes - this section of the beach at Scarborough. The architect came to the project fresh from his triumph at Leeds Town Hall, and his plan, drawn up for the Scarborough Cliff Hotel Company, provided 365 rooms in a colossus of red and yellow brick The Company ran out of money before the job was done, but a Leeds businessman had the pluck to take it on, and see it through to Brodrick's original design. The Grand survives as a hotel despite sundry mishaps and vicissitudes, and stands as a tribute to those who engaged a famous architect and let him have his head. (Simon Hulme/YPN)

In contrast, taken from very much the same place in September 1960, the beach offers unlimited room for castles and dams.

Holidaymakers who have delighted in the resort over very many years would not quibble with this street name. Paradise is indeed to be found in Scarborough. For the shipbuilding Tindalls it must have seemed an ideal address, for they lived there in East Mount House, which they turned into a luxurious dwelling, providing themselves with an Adam dining-room, inlaid mahogany cornices and a garden of an acre or more – Paradise indeed! The Tindalls had launched brigs and baroques from their Scarborough yard from the late 17th Century until 1863, when the building of iron ships sounded the knell for shipbuilders in wood. In 1917, CC Graham, who was Mayor of Scarborough through the years of the Great War, gave East Mount House to the town, and it became the Graham Sea Training School until its students joined the Sea Training Wing of a comprehensive school in 1973. (Mike Cowling/YPN)

This wonderful view of Scarborough shows the way the castle dominates the town. The headland is a natural stronghold, and was occupied by Bronze Age man, the Romans, who built a signal station reputed to have a 100ft tower, and then the Saxons. After the Norman Conquest William le Gros built a castle there that became a Crown possession under Henry II (1133-89). A formidable keep was added during his reign, which began in 1154, and it is the remains of this structure, battered during the Civil War, that now dominate the promontory, bleak, shattered and in the care of English Heritage. (Simon Hulme/YPN)

Scarborough harbour has four piers, including this one, known as Vincent's Pier, which is occupied by the lighthouse, now more than 200 years old. The structure was damaged during the German bombardment in 1914, and rebuilt in the 1930s. (Mike Cowling/YPN)

THE QUEEN OF WATERING PLACES

FROM the 17th Century, Scarborough flourished as a spa, and was eventually endowed (perhaps by Scarborough itself) with the title Queen of Watering Places. The discovery of the source of the hugely profitable waters is attributed to "a discreet gentlewoman", Mrs Elizabeth Farrow. In about 1620, while walking on the beach, she noted that a spring welling from beneath the cliffs had turned stones russet-brown.

She tasted it, found it unpleasant and therefore possibly medicinal, and soon others were trying her "physic". It became invested with curative properties, finding a fervent champion in Dr Robert Wittie of York. Mistress Farrow's discovery was timely, for mineral springs and the wondrous qualities ascribed to them were suddenly all the rage. Bath was flourishing as a spa, with a challenge from Harrogate, where William Slingsby had identified the Tewit Well as a chalybeate spring in 1571.

In his campaign to promote Scarborough, Dr Wittie perceived that the town had one great advantage over its inland rivals. It was able to offer sea-bathing in addition to its waters, thereby affording invalids and hypochondriacs the opportunity of sluicing themselves within and without.

Wittie attracted support. Dr George Tunstall published *Scarborough Spa Spagyrically Anatomised* in 1670, and as a result of this and other efforts the town was soon thriving as a resort. According to an account written in 1734, "it is the custom not only for the gentlemen but the ladies also to bathe in the sea. The gentlemen go out to sea in boats (call'd here cobbles) and jump in naked directly…. the ladies have the convenience of gowns and guides. There are two little houses on the shore to retire to for dressing".

In 1734 Dr Peter Shaw, later Physician in Ordinary to George III, wrote that Scarborough waters, "formerly known to few and healing the sick of inferior rank are … introduced into better company and now cheer the spirits and brace the nerves of Peers as well as commoners". Shaw, who practised and lectured in Scarborough, and therefore can hardly be described as disinterested, prescribed the waters for "diseases of the head, hiccoughs, burning heats and thirsts… common to High Living".

These symptoms bring to mind a hangover, and Scarborough offered facilities whereby such a disability might easily be acquired. By the end of the 18th Century, the town "offered all the refinements of polished life". There were balls every evening, with gentlemen *only* paying for dancing. There was a music gallery, a Pharo-bank, a hazard table, card tables and "raffling and gaming", and the cooks came from London.

One visitor was almost overwhelmed by the Long Room, which he found "very superb… noble", with its 12 chandeliers. On the other hand, the "Spaw Rooms" presented a "naked and scurvy appearance". It seems that the visitors, or "Spaws" as they were known locally, must have been possessed of strong constitutions to withstand this kind of entertainment, as well leaping into shockingly cold sea water every day, and swallowing as many as four pints of spa water.

By the early 19th Century, the town had at least 40 four-wheeled bathing machines. The *New Scarborough Guide* of 1797 described them as "good and roomy", and added that they were in the care of three widows who provided bathing dresses and caps of oiled silk for the ladies. Each bathe cost one shilling and " a gratuity nearly equal to the charge." The machine was drawn into deep water, where a canvas hood, or "tilt", could be dropped over the seaward end to ensure privacy at the moment of entry to the North Sea. Scarborough was among the pioneers of these devices. An engraving by John Setterington dated 1735 shows a kind of hutment on wheels at the brink of the ocean, and is the earliest known depiction of a bathing machine. Also, close inshore, is a boat equipped with an awning from which a bather appears to be emerging.

A typical sea-bathing attendant was caricatured about that time by Thomas Rowlandson as a morose lady wearing an Empire-style blue flannel gown and mobcap. These formidable women "powerfully recommended three immersions", and in some places were known as "Dippers", for their functions included giving apprehensive patrons a helping hand or, if necessary, a good push. John Constable called them "hideous amphibious animals", which seems rather unkind.

The effects of abrupt encounters with the ocean were described in a passage from an unspecified book which Dr OB Appleyard quoted in *The Practitioner* in 1957: "When a healthy person plunges into the sea, he feels a considerable shock or chill… a sobbing succeeds, the skin is contracted and feels rough to the hand, a cracking noise is heard, followed by a ringing or whizzing in the ears, tears sometimes fill the eyes … and many persons experience a little shudder … and later a general glow succeeds and spirits are raised."

Dr Appleyard also recalled that Matthew Bramble, one of the characters created by the Scottish novelist Tobias Smollett, tried bathing at Scarborough and found the waters so chill he could not help "sobbing and bawling out".

Ainsworth's *Guide to Scarborough and its Environs*, which was in its seventh edition by 1832, recommended the waters for various complaints. They "acted gently on the bowels and kidneys", and were beneficial in cases of debility, "relaxations of the stomach", nervous disorders, swelled glands, "particular weakness", and "a variety of chronic complaints, attended by habitual costiveness." However, Ainsworth warned that it was no good to expect wondrous results unless the waters were drunk in Scarborough and at the Spa: "to reap any material advantage, these waters must be drank at the fountain-head; for their virtues, in some measure, depend on an elastic fluid or gas, which quickly escapes from the water; they must necessarily lose some of their properties by being transported to any distance". Thus the guide sought to dissuade those who thought a bottle of water from Scarborough might be as effective as an expensive visit to the town.

 By that time various establishments offered sea water bathing to those reluctant to venture into the ocean, Travis's Baths, Harland's Baths, Champley's Baths and Vickerman's Baths among them. Mrs Farrow's discovery, the main spring of the town's fortunes, suffered "many vicissitudes" according to Theakston in the eighth edition of his *Guide to Scarborough*, published in 1860. In 1737 its outfall was buried by an earthquake, and only recovered after some frantic digging. A violent storm destroyed the building in which it was housed in 1837.

The replacement, built "in the castellated style", and "much admired for its chaste and elegant appearance", opened in August 1839. It was extended in 1847, and ten years later remodelled and

This remarkable view, dating from the late 19th or early 20th Century, shows a forest of sails in the South Bay at Scarborough. In the foreground two horses stand patiently up to their fetlocks in water while barrels are transferred between a cart and a rowing boat.

enlarged to a design by Sir Joseph Paxton, who also laid out Italian gardens in the grounds. The spa then offered the choice of two wells, one known as the north, or chalybeate, and the other as the south, or salt well. Their mineral content was more or less the same, except that the southerly source had slightly greater salinity, as its name indicated.

These wells were housed in a very handsome fashion, to judge from a woodcut of Paxton's Spa that forms the frontispiece to Theakston's *Guide*. However, this structure was damaged by fire, and today's Spa, a grade II listed building, replaced it in 1880, when it was opened by the Lord Mayor of \London. With the architect Cuthbert Brodrick's stupendous Grand Hotel, it is a reminder of the success achieved by the town as a fashionable resort during Victoria's reign.

Somehow the Spa retains a near-indefinable atmosphere of quality and breeding. This may be owed to the sheer style of the Palladian building itself, but here, too, lurk shades of the past, the daring young things of Victorian England who walked the terraces in full-length gowns and engaged in "right down double-barrelled flirting".

The town reached its apogee in October 1871 when the Prince and Princess of Wales came to spend five days as the houseguests of Lord and Lady Londesborough at Londesborough Lodge in The Crescent. A highlight of the visit arrived when the Royal couple joined fashionable crowds at the Spa to hear a recital conducted by Herr Meyer Lutz, who composed a waltz for the occasion. The heir to the throne, then aged 29, and his wife arrived on a Monday and stayed until the following Saturday.

Lord Londesborough had been indisposed during their stay, missing a day's shooting at Grimston, near Tadcaster, and this took on alarming significance as November progressed. The first the public knew of anything untoward was an announcement in the Court Circular of 22nd November that the Prince had been "affected by a sudden indisposition". Ten days later, the Earl of Chesterfield, who had been a fellow-guest at Londesborough Lodge, died of typhoid fever. Lady Londesborough herself had been "much indisposed" for ten days.

The *Yorkshire Post*, among other papers, pointed out that the link between these events was the visit to Scarborough. Lord Londesborough responded by saying that the water supply to the Lodge and the town was pure and excellent. The Lodge sewers had been examined and thoroughly flushed during the visit.

As days passed, the news of the Prince became worse. The gloomy note struck by physicians caused Alfred Austin, the Poet Laureate, to write:

> *Flash'd from his bed, the electric tidings came,*
> *He is no better; he is much the same.*

By December 11th the Queen was told her eldest son would not survive the night, but after 36 hours his fever departed, and he entered a long period of convalescence. Services of thanksgiving were fervent throughout the land, nowhere more so than in Scarborough, which had been in imminent peril of being shunned as the place that poisoned a future King Emperor.

Thereafter Scarborough appointed its first Medical Officer of Health, and a sanitary engineer was engaged to report on the town's drains. No major defect was found, but there was mute

A busy day on Scarborough beach below the Grand Hotel. The men in the foreground all seem to be wearing suits, and some carry umbrellas. It looks sunny, for the children cast shadows. Along the shore, in the middle distance, a horse can be seen pulling a bathing machine out to sea. They had been used at the resort since the early 18th Century, for the first known depiction of such a contraption is in an engraving made there in 1735 by John Setterington.

testimony to the suspicions of the Prince of Wales. He remained friendly with Lord Londesborough, but never returned to Scarborough.

Others did, though, time and again. The guidebook writer George Randolph referred to them with deference as the "upper ten thousand". The common people, he wrote, went to Scarborough to "adore their beauties" and admire the fashionable clothes that it pleased their betters to wear. The Spa terraces, another writer declared, were "thronged with fashionable crowds." Strains of music "always of the best" floated on the air.

By then, Scarborough's transformation into an entertainment centre for the masses was in progress. In 1845 George Hudson's York and North Midland Railway opened a line to the town, and in the refreshment room of the splendidly colonnaded station, by G.T. Andrew of York, new arrivals found a list of lodgings ranging from boarding houses to J.F. Sharpin's Crown Hotel, which was aimed specifically at the "nobility and gentry." However, Hudson, "The Railway King", realised that if his railway was to make a profit, Scarborough would have to appeal to the masses.

With his usual flair he ordered a massive distribution of free tickets to the new destination, thus demonstrating to the teeming population of the West Riding that Scarborough was suddenly and excitingly easy of access. Hudson also looked further afield. Within a month of the opening, there was a cheap trip from Newcastle to Scarborough and back in a day. "What next?" was an admiring newspaper's comment.

One answer to that question was a huge onrush of people. By 1966 Nikolaus Pevsner was quoting one million as the number of annual visitors; the "upper ten thousand", thus swamped, had mostly faded quietly away.

The wealth created by visitors percolated throughout the town, with the exception of one small but significant community: the fisherfolk. In fact, it appears that they became something of an embarrassment as Scarborough pressed its claims to be a resort for the gentry. Theakston's *Guide to Scarborough* simply ignored the contribution of the fishing industry to the wealth of the borough: "The prosperity of Scarborough depends almost entirely on the patronage which is bestowed on it as a watering place".

This seems altogether too sweeping an assertion. Though few in number, Scarborough fishermen made a vast contribution to the wealth of the town, which had been Yorkshire's leading herring port since the Middle Ages, and remained so until the outbreak of the First World War. This was recognised in the mid-13th Century by the grant of Scarborough Fair, made famous by the folk song, which was devoted to the sale of herring, and lasted for 98 days, from 24th June to 29th September.

The trade was of national importance, and offered some protection. Charles II, for example, established a Council of Royal Fishery, and one of its provisions was that all victuallers and coffee-house keepers should buy a barrel of herrings annually, at 30 shillings a barrel.

Huge catches were being made at Scarborough in mid-Victorian times, and fetching good prices. One yawl earned £2,200 over two seasons, 1856 and 1857. In the 1860s the port frequently sent 700-800 tons of herring inland by rail on a single day.

Scarborough led the way in the development of fishing, building the first yawl to come from a Yorkshire yard in 1833. The first purpose-built steam screw trawler, a type of vessel that very quickly replaced the paddle-wheelers that had led steam's challenge to sail, was registered in Scarborough in 1881. Aptly, she was called *Pioneer*, and part-owned by James Sellers, a wealthy wholesaler who also had a financial interest in many fishing vessels.

Yet in some quarters, fishing was regarded as a nuisance. One guide referred loftily to "the honest labouring classes and the fishermen", as if the latter hardly qualified for inclusion in the former. A letter to the *Scarborough Mercury* in 1860 contended that the fish market held on the sands "disgraced this part of town".

Fisherfolk were treated with extraordinary condescension. A visitor to their Primitive Methodist Chapel in St Sepulchre Street wrote in 1865 that one of their number preached "rudely but earnestly" to a congregation made up chiefly of fellow seamen. Theakston's *Guide* lamented disturbances occasioned by the conflicts within the waterfront community, and called for the conviction of offenders. This was a reference to occasional bouts of fisticuffs, resulting in cracked heads, broken bones and other injuries that erupted from time to time.

These ructions were usually prompted by conflict between herring smacksmen and trawlermen. The troubles can be traced back to the arrival in 1831 of two south country trawlers whose landings flooded the market, depressing prices. This infuriated locals, who gathered in an attempt to prevent the "foreigners" landing their catch. There were more disturbances the following year, causing the town's magistrates to swear in preventive men as special constables.

The problems caused by the introduction of trawling were recognised nationally. An Act of Parliament granted Royal Assent in August 1843 was intended "to carry into effect a convention between Her Majesty and the King of the French concerning the Fisheries in the Seas between the British Islands and France". This forbade the use of trawl nets within three miles of a sea area where herring were being netted.

The Act also provided that fishing boats should be numbered for ready identification. The law seems to have been difficult to enforce, and, according to Theakston, trawlers frequently made prohibited passage across the herring grounds and "if they come into contact with a drift or herring net which ..... might impede their progress, no scruple is made to cut it in twain and cast it adrift." Also, "after the fashion of pirates or smugglers", trawlermen would obscure their ship's number with a piece of canvas.

This kind of behaviour inevitably caused trouble ashore and afloat. An example, quoted by Theakston, concerned R. Wyvill of Scarborough, who was presumably a relative of Henry Wyvill, a sailor who became a fish wholesaler and, like James Sellers, either bought or took shares in fishing boats. Wyvill encountered a marauding trawling smack, and was hailed by its master, who demanded that the herring nets impeding his progress be cut or cast adrift.

In reply, Wyvill demanded the rival's name and number, and "not being answered, he very boldly took his lesser boat, and in the face of a rough sea, hastened on board the trawler, determined there to remain until he had discovered and could prosecute the offender".

This bold act on the high seas would probably have appealed to the founding-fathers of modern Scarborough, the men who gave the borough its name. For many years, it was thought to be Saxon in origin, from "scaur" meaning rock, and "burg", a fortress. There were doubts about this, though, and a different theory evolved through the combined scholarship of Professor EV Gordon of Leeds

University, and a colleague, Professor AH Smith, who was an accepted authority on Yorkshire place names.

The two academics studied Scandinavian invasions of this country, and traced the history of two brothers, Thorgills Skarthi and Kormak, who raided the east coast from Scotland to the Wash. According to the new theory, the brothers established a base at Scarborough, making it likely that the town's name sprang from "Skarthi's Stronghold", Skarthi being a nickname for "hare-lip".

The year of the coming of these warlike seafarers was given as 966, and in 1966 Scarborough celebrated its own Millennium, with the lugubrious sound of sheep's horns in the street, "son et lumiere" at the castle, a square rigger in the bay, and even the enactment of a Viking funeral on the beach.

No doubt some form of township existed when the brothers arrived and led their men to the Castle mound, a hill that stands out like a boss on the coastline, and would be the first sight of land for successive waves of invaders.

Archaeological excavations on the summit yielded evidence that a community lived there in the Bronze Age and early Iron Age. From fragments of pottery, tools, harness rings and pins the idea evolved that its inhabitants were warriors from Holland or the Rhineland, who arrived some 700 to 800 years BC. Later came occupation by the Romans, and their establishment of signal stations along the coast.

One of the key links in this chain of watchtowers was built on Castle Mound. Excavations before the First World War revealed foundations that enabled experts to deduce that a wooden tower some 100ft in height once stood at the brow of the promontory. This was abandoned during the Romans' withdrawal from Britain, and with their protective arm removed, sea wolves prowled the coast.

The character of these Norseman emerges with clarity from their sagas. A Northumbrian earl's lament at the prospect of dying a "cow's death" in his bed is typical of the Viking. No doubt he would have preferred to be cut down in battle, a sword in hand and a battle-cry on his lips. Thorkelin the Dane chronicled an expedition led by a couple who may sound like a comedy duo today, Knut and Gorm, but who must have been no kind of joke to their 10th Century victims, including people living in what came to be Scarborough.

The tendency was for the invaders to colonise the land they seized, and there is plenty of evidence of this in the North Riding's place-names, its folklore, and even the speech of its inhabitants, for many dialect words can be traced back to Scandinavia. According to Oswald Harland's *Yorkshire-North Riding* (Robert Hale, 1951) old dialectical forms persisted among Scarborough fisherfolk until the Second World War, chiefly the use of the unblurred initial *d* for *th* in words like *those, this, these, the and there*. At the same time, Mr Harland noted that the families who had lived for generations in the older part of town, the Owstons, Cammishes, Sheaders and Capplemans, were dwindling in numbers.

About a century after the brothers Thorgills, Skarthi and Kormac had settled at Scarborough, there was a further invasion from the sea. Earl Tostig and Harold Hardrada, King of Norway, who were eventually defeated by Canute at Stamford Bridge, sailed into the bay with a fleet reputed to number 300 ships.

They encountered resistance from townsfolk, who probably lived in wooden dwellings clad with thatch, grouped round Castle Hill. Hardrada, fighting under his banner, "The Landwaster", seized the summit, and, according to Snorri Sturlasson's Saga, "caused an immense pile of wood to be raised and set on fire". Brands were plucked from this blaze and hurled down the hill to land among the houses below. Flames spread from one to another, and the defenders were flushed from their refuges to die at the hands of the invading army.

Scarborough was virtually obliterated; there is no reference to the town in the Domesday survey of 1086, although "Walsgrif" (Falsgrave) is mentioned. With the Normans in control after Hastings, a castle soon protected the mound. It was initiated by William le Gros, Earl of Albermarle and York, who in 1138 won a great victory over the Scots at the Battle of the Standard, near Northallerton. By then he had started fortifying Castle Rock, which, according to the Chronicler of the Abbey of Meaux in the East Riding, was "a very costly work".

The fortification was to dominate the town and its history for five centuries, and was fought over in earnest several times, notably during the Civil War, when Sir Hugh Cholmley held it for Parliament in a siege that began in February 1645. Bombarded from sea and land, the defenders held out with the utmost gallantry until July 1645, when disease and shortage of water caused Cholmley to surrender. Following further brief Royalist defiance in 1648, the Council of State of the Commonwealth ordered the castle's demolition. By then, however, Scarborough was set on another course, its development as a spa.

FISHERFOLK AT WORK

According to the original caption, this is "a Runswick fisherwoman sewing". That is as may be, but she is certainly wearing what would today be called a Staithes bonnet. This illustrates the point that such bonnets were not unique to Staithes. At one time they would be commonplace in all the fishing communities, part of the essential working dress along with long skirts, hessian or cotton aprons, and shawls for warmth. A bonnet takes a yard of cotton and was a practical garment, protecting the neck, and with a double-crown due to the weight the fisher wives and lasses carried on their heads. In mourning, a black bonnet was worn, and at Staithes it was not considered the done thing to revert immediately to white when the mourning period was over. Instead, according to a memory collected by the East Cleveland Heritage Project Oral History Team, the women went into mauve bonnets.

Yorkshire Post *and* Yorkshire Evening Post *photographers like Wilbur Wright, George Stott, Harry Fletcher and Bill Hirst always had a ready lens for a picture illustrating working life along the coast, as this and the following pictures demonstrate..*
With the herring season at its height, nets needed constant attention. In August 1965 Ken Crawford was getting to grips with a tangle on the fish quay at Scarborough.

Nets under repair at Bridlington in 1954.

Examining a net at Goole in 1941.

Maintaining crab pots is an essential job for these two old fishermen at Goole in 1941.

Crab pots need dousing in creosote or a similar preservative if they are to survive a season in the North Sea. At Bridlington in 1956, pots are being prepared for use on the coble.

BILLY BUTLIN'S HOLIDAY CAMP

BILLY Butlin was born in 1899 in South Africa, but moved with his parents to Canada. He served in the First World War, and afterwards worked his passage to England with only a fiver to his name. He worked for a time in a fun fair, and was inspired with the idea of providing cheap holidays for the masses, with decent accommodation, good food and plenty of entertainment. He opened his first camp at Skegness in 1936, followed by another at Clacton in 1938. He settled on Yorkshire as the site for a third, and carried out a personal investigation.

How he settled on Filey was explained by Ethel Milner, then aged 97, in the Remember Filey Butlins Project, set up in 2005 with a grant of £43,900 from the Heritage Lottery Fund. Drawing on her wonderful memory, she told Alan Micklethwaite, who recorded her story for the Project, that it had been her father who sold Butlin the land on which he built his camp.

George Milner farmed at Hunmanby Gap, and Billy Butlin first set eyes on his holding during an exploratory visit to the Primrose Valley caravan site. He looked over a hedge and remarked: "There's some lovely land over there".

Subsequently his agent made an offer to Mr Milner for part of his acreage, which was called Moor Farm. Miss Milner said her father wanted time to think, and put off making a decision for a month. He eventually sold 120 acres at £100 an acre - £12,000. "We never had such money," said Miss Milner, "but we did not celebrate. We didn't do anything daft like that". Instead the Milners got on with farming their remaining land, extending to 189 acres.

Butlin won support for his plan from Filey Town Council in 1939, but soon after work started war broke out and all three camps were requisitioned. At Filey, this was a blessing, albeit in heavy disguise, for according to Miss Milner, the Government carried on and built Billy Butlin's camp for him, chalets and all. No doubt he kept a friendly eye on progress in his wartime role as director-general of hostels to the Ministry of Supply.

Filey was in the holiday business surprisingly quickly after the end of the war. At a time of severe shortages, Billy Butlin managed to get construction work done What had been the parade ground for men of the RAF Regiment serving at RAF Hunmanby Moor (the camp's wartime designation) became a boating lake A spur was added to the Hull-Scarborough railway line that passed under the road in a tunnel and delivered holidaymakers to a new station opened in May 1947, only a couple of years after VE-Day.

As the camp thrived, it drew in large numbers of part-time workers. I remember that in 1948 or 1949 two or three girls in the sixth form of Whitby Grammar School announced they had holiday jobs there, and would be staying on site. We had heard rumours of chalet-hopping and quizzed them eagerly on their return, but they dismissed us as a lot of grubby-minded boys, and said everybody behaved like perfect gentlemen. Ho-hum we thought, recalling the activities of certain gentlemen of our acquaintance at RV Hindmarsh's Royal Hotel, Whitby, where the Silver Stars band played for dancing on Saturday evenings, but it was probably all very innocent, sex not having been

These two pictures encompass the history of Butlin's Holiday Camp at Filey. In the first, taken by a Yorkshire Post *photographer in June 1946, the camp is incomplete. In the second, taken in 1967, it is at the peak of its popularity. Accommodating up to 10,000 campers, it employed 1,500 staff, and was of huge importance in the local economy.*

invented in those days.

Butlin's, despite its transient population, assumed an air of permanence, and it was difficult to believe it was closing for ever when its owners decided to pull out and put it on the market in 1983, three years after the death of the founder, by then Sir Billy Butlin.

The site has been a sorry mess for much of the time since, but the Remember Filey Butlins Project built up a wonderful archive of memories of the place in its pomp that is now preserved at Bridlington Central Library.

A train has delivered a new crowd of holidaymakers eager to sample the delights of Butlin's, Filey. Waiting to take them to their chalets is the camp's own train.

Lord Middleton declares the new Filey Holiday Camp station open, 10th May 1947.

'CLIMMIN' AT BEMPTON

MEN from the Flamborough area harvested eggs from the cliffs at Bempton for generations, working together in gangs of five. As many as 130,000 guillemot eggs were said to have been taken in a single year towards the end of the 19th Century, although another estimate put the total collection at about 60,000 to 70,000 per season. Some eggs were eaten, those laid by kittiwakes being much favoured by gourmets. Others were sold to collectors, and many went to Leeds, where they were used in the manufacture of patent leather.

Collection from the cliffs – "climming" - was specifically excluded from provisions of the Sea Birds' Protection Act, which reached the statute book in June 1869. This afforded protection for 35 species by imposing a close season from 1st April to 1st August, and was aimed at the large number of "sportsmen" who shot at the birds from boats.

These vessels, mainly from Bridlington, sailed close to the cliffs and sounded their hooters to scare the birds from their nests. As they rose, guns were fired indiscriminately into the white ascending clouds, and great slaughter was achieved. As a result, eggs were left unhatched, and young birds starved.

It was mainly purposeless killing, although some plumage found its way into ladies' hats. Razorbills, fulmars, puffins, kittiwakes and all the rest found a champion in Christopher Sykes (1831-1898), brother of Sir Tatton Sykes of Sledmere, the fifth baronet. He was MP for Beverley, and then the East Riding, for 27 years, but made only six speeches and asked but three questions.

However, prompted by local naturalists, he did stir himself on behalf of the birds to good effect, for his Act put paid to the pot-shot mariners at a stroke.

The practice of "climming" continued for another three-quarters of a century without any apparent diminution in the number of seabirds nesting at Bempton, estimated at about 200,000. It was eventually outlawed by the Protection of Birds Act in 1954, leaving the birds in peril only from our poisoning the seas and our emptying them of fish.

Egg collecting on Bempton cliffs was not a job for the faint-hearted, as this picture taken in May 1946 shows. The man on the end of the line was preparing to swing back in, seize a crevice in the chalk face with one hand, and use the other to collect eggs and place them in a bag slung round his shoulder.

The man on the rope was not without support. This picture, taken in 1945, shows four stalwarts bracing themselves to ensure their colleague's safety. To the left is a wicker basket full of eggs. The "climmers" were not so much afraid of falling down the sheer cliffs as of dislodged rocks tumbling on their heads. As a precaution, some wore top hats or billycocks stuffed with cotton-wool or horsehair.

No wonder there is much hilarity among these folk at the cliff top in May 1946.
To judge from the trophy held by the "climmer", emus had joined the nesting colony on Bempton cliffs.

Wartime tin hats were in fashion for "climmers" by the time this picture was taken in 1946 of a successful return to the welcoming group at the cliff top.

BRIDLINGTON AND THE ENTERPRISING MR MILNE

THE Gypsey Race reaches the sea at Bridlington, and thus may be numbered among that town's many charms, for it is a wayward stream, the subject of many curious tales.

According to the Ordnance Survey map it rises in a field about half-a-mile to the west of a great antiquity of the Yorkshire Wolds, the prehistoric burial mound called Duggleby Howe. Sure enough, when we went on an exploratory expedition, it was there, bubbling merrily away through thick grass. It was soon in a culvert under a road leading down from Wharram-le-Street before heading off on its 20-odd mile journey to the sea.

My wife and I had set ourselves the task that day of following this most capricious of streams down the Great Wold Valley, that deep green fold in the landscape anciently known as Grindalythe. The Race is perhaps the best known of all the "gypsies" (sometimes "gipsies"), the streams that drain the chalky uplands of the Wolds, flowing intermittently and sometimes running for a distance underground.

They owe their character to the underlying chalk, which is an aquifer, or body of water-bearing rock. When this porous chamber fills, which may not follow immediately after rain, for it is a leisurely process, the water surfaces and the streams flow. In places man has intervened, drawing water for irrigation, perhaps, or putting in drains, and the East Yorkshire Chalk Rivers Trust has been set up by volunteers anxious for the well-being of Wolds chalk streams, many of which eventually find their way to the Hull river.

We tracked the Race through Duggleby, and among the humps in a field marking the site of Mowthorpe, one of the lost villages of the East Riding. It plunged on through fields of corn, and ran alongside the lane leading to Kirby Grindalyth church with its Norman tower and, inside, an astonishing 19th Century Italian mosaic.

This, like much else in churches round the Wolds, was placed there at the behest of Sir Tatton Sykes, the 5th Baronet. It may originally have been intended for the chapel at Sledmere House by Sir Tatton's wife, Lady Jessie, who converted to Roman Catholicism and from whom he eventually became estranged. By whatever means it reached Kirkby Grindalyth, the depiction of Our Lord's Ascension in tesserae is a rare embellishment for an English country church.

By then the Race's flow was sufficient to register several notches on a depth indicator, and came near to justifying the title of river. But it is no end of a tease, and a short distance down the valley, at West Lutton, it was a mere stream again, squirting from a field to enter a conduit under the road. At nearby Helperthorpe, where it rushed under a series of small bridges linking cottages with the highway, it ran in sufficient strength to flood a ford.

Only another mile further on, at Weaverthorpe, it had absented itself altogether. We stared in surprise at an empty bed where the mud had cracked into strange shapes under a hot sun. Butterwick was dry, but the Race was flowing again at Wold Newton, a village with two large ponds. Its progress was legarthic, and it appeared to be nearly stagnant as it passed beneath a bridge on the road to Thwing.

Sure enough, it did not make it to Burton Fleming, the next village. Its course alongside the green was grassed over, and bright with daisies and dandelions. Water, surely, had not run there for a long time. For quite a distance hereabouts, the Race habitually runs underground, only emerging to twinkle in the light of day at times of flood. Beyond Burton Fleming, where the Race suddenly heads south to Rudston before making its final turn to Bridlington, there was nothing to see but wet mud, a calling card left by a river that had again slipped into temporary oblivion.

Superstitious folk viewed the appearance and disappearance of "gypsies" as portents, and not good ones either, as their other name, "woe waters", indicates. The Gypsey Race is credited with forecasting the execution of Charles I, the Great Plague, the landing of Prince William of Orange, the assassination of Archduke Ferdinand in 1914, and much else beside. A chronicler in 1622, probably anticipating murrain at the very least, recorded gloomily that it had "fallen into the earth".

Attempts have been made here and there to coerce it into consistent behaviour by creating channels, but to no avail. The Gypsey Race still comes and goes as it pleases.

It reaches the sea at what used to be known as Bridlington Quay to distinguish the waterside from the older town, with its quaint High Street, that is a distance inland. Bridlington's natural advantages as a holiday resort are manifold, for it is sited on the shore of a magnificent bay fringed by beautiful beaches. Sea bathing began to become popular in the mid-18th Century, and was eagerly promoted by Dr Richard Russell, whose *Dissertation on the use of Sea-water* was published in 1750.

This recommended sea-water as a general cure-all and was a runaway success. Taking the plunge was not intended to be pleasurable, and early advocates suggested winter as the time when indulgence would produce the best results. Bridlington was well placed to entertain those who wished to adopt this fashion, and wealthy bathers began to arrive in the second half of the 18th Century, perhaps preferring the town's calm atmosphere to the social round of Scarborough. .

The providential tapping of a well of fresh water kindled hopes of further development as a fashionable resort. A stone was placed nearby bearing the inscription: "This tidal spring was discovered on the 3rd July, 1811, by Benjamin Milne, collector of customs, Bridlington". Contemporary accounts went into more detail:

He discovered *"the striking phenomenon of an ebbing and flowing spring of fine fresh water in the harbour, and in order to keep open (the flow) a pipe three inches in diameter was sunk from the surface to the source. At full tide the spring water stands in the perpendicular tube eight feet above the level of the sea water in the harbour, and is so pure and soft that it is used in the washing of the finest linen."*

Milne's discovery was made during harbour-improvement work, and the well was tapped at a depth of about 40ft

Bridlington no doubt hoped that the water thus released might prove as effective a prophylactic as those from wells at Scarborough and Harrogate, which were supposed to cure just about every ailment known to man. Alas, the harbour spring lacked any great infusion of chemicals and was of remarkable purity. The water was not, however, allowed to run to waste. It was piped in a copper tube and stored in a reservoir "constructed for the use of the town and its shipping". Bridlington's washerwomen were presumably able to launder with it, and to achieve an early version of whiter than white.

Walter White, who visited the resort while compiling his *A Month in Yorkshire* (1858), categorised Milne's discovery as an artesian well, and also reported a chalybeate spring bursting from the cliff to the north of the harbour. Black's *Picturesque Guide* (1867) contained an enthusiastic review of Bridlington Quay, "a favourite resort for sea-bathing and its mineral water", and declared that its chalybeate water was like that of Cheltenham and Scarborough "but perhaps with less of salts in its ingredients".

Even so, a guide of 1860 asserted that "persons afflicted with lithic disorders have been greatly relieved". This is a reference to lithiasis, the formation of stones in the human body, especially in the bladder, undoubtedly a very painful condition. But the modest claim did not promise a cure, so it would hardly draw "Spaws"(the name given to folk who took the waters) in great numbers like Harrogate, say, or Cheltenham.

Benjamin Milne served Bridlington well during his years there, from 1791 until his death in 1819. He arranged for the town to have a daily post, and encouraged the building of the first public baths. Nearby, at Flamborough, he had an important part in persuading the Brethren of Trinity House to adopt his proposal for a lighthouse. He was probably inspired to this endeavour by the terrible toll of ships and sailors exacted by Flamborough Head, where 174 vessels were lost in the years 1770-1806. Once the light shone, the number of wrecks reduced dramatically.

After his death, a Bridlington contemporary composed a poetic tribute:

> *"Is Milne forgotten? His works answer No!*
> *And their voice, like the voice of the loud-sounding deep,*
> *Shall be heard, whilst its waters continue to flow"*

There is more in the same vein. Doggerel it may be, but the writer had a valid point. Benjamin Milne is not forgotten.

The older part of Bridlington includes the Priory Church, which contains some fragments of the monastic house established by Augustinian Canons in the early 12th Century. The only monastic building to survive is the Gatehouse, or Bayle, built in about 1390, which is now a museum.

In the churchyard lie many of the victims of the great gale of 1871, a stunning catastrophe. Strong winds early that month had penned a fleet of some 400 vessels, mainly collier brigs laden with coals for London, in north-east coast ports. The weather then eased, tempting them to put to sea, and by February 9th, when many of them had rounded Flamborough Head and reached Bridlington Bay, the wind fell away altogether. Their crews must have congratulated themselves on being becalmed in the so-called "Bay of Safety".

However, in the small hours of 10th February a furious storm sprang upon them from the southeast. It was soon blowing a hurricane, and many of the colliers were trapped against a lee shore, unable to beat to windward. Some made a dash towards the beach, hoping to reach safety

Bridlington's great lifeboat tradition goes back to 1805, when a boat was purchased by public subscription. From its foundation in 1824, the Royal National Lifeboat Institution has had a boat on service. This picture shows a launch in November 1947.

A tractor hauling the lifeboat down the slipway for a launch off the beach at Bridlington in 1965.

through the surf. Others, seeking to ride out the storm, dragged their anchors and were hurled to destruction by the North Sea, whose reputation as a widow-maker was most horribly justified that day. Soon two lifeboats, the rocket life-saving brigade, coastguards and volunteers were attempting to pluck survivors form the wrecks. As five vessels came ashore almost simultaneously to the north side of the harbour, more help was needed, and virtually the entire town turned out to attempt to assist in rescues, and cheer on those who were doing so. The lifeboatmen performed heroics, but the Royal National Lifeboat Association's *Robert Whitworth*, had to be taken out of service. Her crew had saved 12 lives from three wrecks, but they were exhausted. Their hands were raw with cold and lacerated after an epic two-hour attempt to get alongside a merchantman that eventually went down with all hands.

That left the *Harbinger*, a smaller boat, which had been made skilfully in mahogany by David Purdon, at the expense of a Hungarian nobleman living in the town. She was known as the "Fishermen's Lifeboat", and she went out seven times with relays of volunteers at the oars. Answering yet another call, David Purdon himself and his assistant, John Clappison, joined the crew.

Attempting to reach an elderly man clinging to the rigging of the Whitby brig *Delta*, the lifeboat capsized. She righted herself, but six of her crew drowned, including David Purdon and John Clappison. As the town went into mourning, the cries of more drowning men were lost in the tumult of the storm. From the beach, sailors could be seen clinging to the rigging of wrecks, but they could not be saved, and they disappeared one by one.

The RNLI reckoned 70 men were drowned that day and 40 vessels lost. An extraordinary photograph taken at the time shows the beach deep in wreckage, spars, smashed boats, tattered sails, discarded sea boots, and quantities of coal.

Bridlington raised up a monument to the lifeboatmen and "a great company of seamen" in the Priory churchyard. For a century afterwards the anniversary of the catastrophe was commemorated on "Storm Sunday", with a lifeboat hauled through the streets and a turnout of the Mayor and Corporation, and the occasion is still recalled each year during morning service on the nearest Sunday to February 10th.

STORMY SEAS

SHAKESPEARE, as usual, had words for it: "…as hungry as the sea, and can digest so much." This sequence of photographs shows the necessity for lifeboats such as that at Bridlington. It also depicts the North Sea at its most greedy, and some of the consequences of its appetite. It has gobbled up many acres of Holderness, where the land is boulder clay, but it also takes bites out of rocky cliffs. Whitby Abbey, for example is much closer to the brink than it was when Norman monks re-settled the headland nearly 1,000 years ago.

The great storms illustrated by this series of photographs, mostly taken by *Yorkshire Post* photographers, can provide the ocean with a sudden feast, great quantities of earth and rock, but the process of erosion is more a matter of nibbling away on every tide, especially the Springs.

The sequence begins at Sandsend in March 1958, with a member of the North Riding Constabulary observing some unruly behaviour along the sea front.

The same location in the aftermath of a devastating storm, showing the extent to which the North Sea is capable of powering its way through sea defences.

Two wonderful pictures on Scarborough sea front in 1958. One shows a crowd of spectators keeping a sensible distance, while in the other a couple of Morris Minors and a Ford saloon would have been lucky to escape the descent of a towering wall of water.

This atmospheric picture was taken at Bridlington in 1963. It shows an unfriendly, lowering sky, and a big breaker spending itself against the shore.

The effect of heavy weather on the vulnerable coast is demonstrated by this shot. It was taken at Barmston, near Bridlington, in 1969, and the North Sea has extracted yet more land, leaving a nice old street lamp balanced precariously, and what appears to be a large section of concrete upended half-way down the cliff.

KINGSTON-UPON-HULL – "ONELY BULWARKE OF THE NORTH" *

KING Edward I, who reigned from 1272 to 1307, chose the old town of Wyke, where the sinuous River Hull joins the Humber, as the site of a Royal arsenal on the northern shore of the Humber estuary. It was already a port, busy with fishing and the export of wool, when the King acquired its site from the Cistercian monks of Meaux in exchange for other lands, keeping them waiting 11 years for a final settlement.

He granted the townsmen a charter in 1299, bestowing on them the privileges of a "Free Borough", a twice-weekly market, and an annual 30-day fair.

Edward I became known as the "Hammer of the Scots", and this was inscribed on his tomb in Westminster Abbey in the Latin version, *Scotorum malleus*. . He used Hull as a supply port during his Scottish campaigns, and looked to the town to furnish him with ships and men for various Royal adventures.

His heir, Edward II, who succeeded to the throne in 1307, continued to favour his father's choice of Hull as a northern supply depot, and in 1321 he licensed defensive works consisting of a ditch and a crenellated wall surrounding the town. Some 4,500,000 bricks went into the construction, which enclosed 80 acres and had four gateways. No doubt urgency was added by events in October 1322, when the Scots, under Robert the Bruce, conquered Edward's army in the Battle of Byland. The King fled to York, leaving behind the Crown Jewels and many of his nobles, who were held hostage. He eventually took refuge at the Royal Manor of Burstwick, near Hull, and the Scots, not far behind, rampaged across the Wolds, and came as close as Beverley.

Through the 14th Century, Kingston-upon-Hull flourished. A marvellous medley of goods was being imported from the mainland of Europe. From Norway came falcons for the King, together with timber, oil, litmus and furs. From the Baltic came more timber, pitch, tar and ashes, corn, beer, eels and sturgeon. From Gascony came wine, often making up a complete cargo.

Hull became a notable centre of the wine trade, and developed the pleasing habit of making gifts of choice vintages to those in positions of influence and power, the Earl of Northumberland, for example, and noblemen like the Lords Clifford, Neville, Salisbury and Buckingham.

Hull merchants accumulated fortunes. The most prominent were William de la Pole and his sons Richard and William. Richard became the Royal wine merchant, and he and William acted as bankers to the Crown. In 1332, five years after he had acceded to the throne, Edward III, whose long reign of 50 years began in 1327 when he was only 14 years of age, visited Hull as the guest of William de la Pole, and dubbed his host knight.

* *The quotation is from a poem by John Taylor (1580-1653), "The Water-Poet", and is part of his "A Very Merry Wherry-Ferry Voyage", in a collection published in 1630.*

He also granted the townsfolk the right to a Mayor, and Sir Richard was the first to hold this office. Your may see an alabaster effigy of this great man, who was styled "Our well-beloved merchant" and founded a noble dynasty, in Holy Trinity Church at Hull. His son Michael was Mayor in his turn in 1376, and went on to be Lord Chancellor of England and the first Earl of Suffolk. One of his grandsons raised his banner at Agincourt alongside that of Henry V, and a great-grandson married into the Royal family, taking the sister of Edward IV as his bride.

In old Hull stands a handsome two-storey Georgian building with a striking pediment bearing the Royal Arms supported by Neptune and Britannia. It is the headquarters of the Brethren of the "Guild or Fraternity of Masters and Pilots, Seamen of the Trinity House of Kingston upon Hull", known popularly as Trinity House or, yet more simply, The House.

Originally formed in 1369 as the Guild of the Holy Trinity, membership of this ancient institution has since 1457 been restricted to master mariners and pilots. But there are also Honorary Brethren, notable for their service to the city or the country. The Duke of Edinburgh currently heads the list.

The dignified interior is full of interest. Preserved there is the axe used by the Haven Master of the 17th Century to cut the mooring lines of ships in breach of his berthing orders. Relics of Captain Cook include weapons of the South Seas that he brought home from his voyages, and the armchair from his cabin. Among the many ship-models is one for which a sailor used his own hair to make the rigging.

Trinity House has been a lively institution for more than six centuries, engaged in charitable work and education. In its prime business, maritime matters, its responsibilities ranged from the pilotage of the Humber to the provision of lights to aid navigation in the estuary

The first Spurn lifeboat went on station in October 1810. The Brethren had launched a subscription list to buy a boat while Francis Constable, Lord of the Manor of Spurn, undertook to provide a residence for the master of the lifeboat, and twelve Kilnsea men to form the crew.

The master was expected to be able to support himself by managing a tavern that would be built on the point, and selling provisions to vessels that called there to take on ballast. In addition, he was to be supplied with coal, candles, a spyglass, a flagstaff and flag, and six casks for the storage of fresh water.

These facts and many more are stored in the records of the House, and were drawn on freely by Arthur Storey for his fascinating Trinity House of Kingston upon Hull, *published by Trinity House itself in 1967.*

This glance at the trade of Medieval Hull might convey the impression of unbroken prosperity. But in 1461, when the Wars of the Roses had emptied the municipal coffers, the town's creditors could only be pacified by taking up the main water conduit and doling out lead to them. It was rather like presenting the plumbing to the bailiffs.

Despite its comparative isolation, Hull has never been far from the mainstream of English history. Henry VIII's visit in 1541 resulted in the construction of the citadel on the eastern bank of the River Hull, thus underlining its importance as a garrison town and Royal arsenal.

Perhaps its most dramatic moment came in 1642, when Charles I (1600-1649) found the city gates shut in his face. Like the Parliamentarians, he was anxious to secure arms and ammunition held behind the walls of the "King's Town", but when he arrived on 23rd April he was refused entry. Sir John Hotham, the Governor, appeared on the battlements, and said he was very sorry to disobey the King's command, but he "durst not open the gates to him, being intrusted by the Parliament with the safety of the town". Various palavers seem to have gone on for five hours, but Sir John remained obdurate, whereupon the exasperated King had heralds proclaim him guilty of high treason before riding off to Beverley. In the following August, Charles raised his banner at Nottingham, signalling the start of the Civil War.

Both protagonists on that April day outside Hull suffered the same fate. Charles I was beheaded in Whitehall, London, in January 1649, and Sir John Hotham was likewise deprived on Tower Hill, London, in 1645. He and his son, Captain Hotham, had been accused of "traitorously betraying the trust imposed on them by Parliament" by plotting to give Kingston-upon-Hull to King Charles's wife, Queen Henrietta Maria. She had been fund-raising on her husband's behalf on the Continent, and eventually landed at Bridlington in February 1643, bringing with her a sum reputed to amount to £2m. The Hothams apparently turned their coats because Sir John felt he had been slighted when Parliament chose another Yorkshireman, Lord Halifax, to command their forces in the north.

Hull's transformation from a small medieval township to the third port in the kingdom, crucial to the well-being of the nation, took place in the 18th and early 19th Centuries. As the West Riding benefited from the Industrial Revolution, so, too, did Hull. Textiles from the proliferating wool mills continued as the main source of exports, but it also became the chief outlet for the cutlery, tools, stoves, grates, and other hardware produced in south Yorkshire. Initially, the only wharfage available was in the lower reach of the Hull river, known as the Haven. As trade increased, it proved woefully inadequate, and in 1774 the Hull Dock Company was formed, Britain's first statutory undertaking of its kind. Its Queen's Dock was so successful that by 1786 there was agitation for yet more wharfage.

Shipbuilding was booming, and it is impossible to study the years 1770-1835 without thrilling to the excitement of a city thrusting itself to the forefront, due largely to the enterprise of individuals. Many were innovators. Horace B Browne, in his *Story of the East Riding of Yorkshire* (1912), told of two men, Messrs Furness and Ashton, who built England's first steamboat in their yard at Wincolmlee in 1787, and launched it in the river Hull. The engine was patented in the following year, and the makers later built a larger steamboat that was assembled in London. It was bought by the Prince Regent (later King George IV), who rewarded Furness and Ashton with a pension of £70 each.

Hugh Blaydes built warships for the Royal Navy and helped place Hull among the country's three biggest shipbuilders. Joseph Pease opened the first of his mills for the extraction of oil from rapeseed in 1740, and went into banking. William Osbourne (sometime Osborne), a timber merchant and saw-miller, bought a Scottish forest for £20,000 and was said to have "made at least double off it." He was apparently in partnership with a man called Dodsworth, and in 1784 they signed a contract with the Duke of Gordon to buy all the timber in the Duke's extensive forest of Glenmore. When they set up in business, the mouth of the Spey, on the Moray Firth near Elgin, was merely shingle and marsh, but Osbourne and Dodsworth developed a township there that they named Kingston-on-Spey, and set about building ships, big vessels of 500 tons, with 60ft masts.

By the early 1800s their yards were producing clipper ships, sleek ocean racers designed for the Indian tea trade. Their endeavours were viewed with some awe by the locals, one of whom wrote: "The log and spars belonging to the English company are at times floated down the River Spey in single pieces, in number perhaps 20,000 at a time, and they are conducted by 50 to 80 men going along the sides of the river to push them off by poles as they stick to the banks". The men were hired at a halfpenny a day "and a competent allowance of spirituous liquor".

James Hamilton, a whale oil merchant, sent his ship, *York*, to Greenland in 1754 and thus opened a vastly prosperous fishery that lasted more than a century, for it was not until 1868 that the *Truelove*, whose ancient timbers had braved the Arctic seas on 72 occasions, made Hull's last whaling voyage. She docked in the autumn of that year with a cargo of 760 seals that produced nine tons of oil, a modest return compared with the peak years of 1818 and 1819, when Hull sent a fleet of 64 vessels to Greenland and the Davis Strait.

Truelove would be among them. She was the Humber's most famous ship, a three-masted barque built at Philadelphia, USA, in 1764. She was captured by the Royal Navy during the American war, and sold to a Hull merchant. Her first whaling voyage was to Spitzbergen in 1784. After her last visit to the Arctic, she continued in service as a merchantman, and in 1873, by then in her 109th year, visited Philadelphia, where her captain and crew were given an enthusiastic welcome. She continued making trading voyages to Scandinavia, but was eventually broken up as unseaworthy.

The inheritors of the hard seagoing traditions of the whaling crews quickly turned to deep sea trawling. The first vessel fitted out for this type of fishing had arrived in Hull in 1854, and local seamen changed their quarry from whales and seals to cod and halibut. In 1840 there had been only seven fishing vessels registered at Hull, mostly shrimpers. By 1883 the port's fish trade was reckoned to provide employment for 20,000 people, and the Hessle Road area was already known for its fishing community. Huge catches were being made in the North Sea. The Great Silver Pit, to the south of the Dogger Bank, yielded large quantities of sole, with as many as 18,000 pairs being landed on a single day during the hard winter of 1844-1845. This prodigious harvest attracted West Country fishing smack owners, among them the Hellyers, who came from Brixham, and established one of the major trawler-owning companies on the Humber.

Such enterprises brought great benefits. In the last quarter of the 18th Century the suburbs were spilling beyond the walls of the old town, and in the 30 years from 1801 the population increased by 69 per cent. Nor was it altogether a workaday community committed to toil. William

Wilberforce called it "one of the gayest places outside London". Tate Wilkinson, who managed the new Theatre Royal when it opened in 1810, wrote that "Hull, for hospitality and plenty of good cheer" was entitled to call itself "the Dublin of England".

The port developed as the natural centre for a system of inland waterways, but was less happily placed for railways, being cut off from the south by the Humber, and lying 35 miles from the East Coast main line at York. Hull's first railway, opened in 1840, ran to Selby where it linked up with a line to Leeds. This service fell into the hands of George Hudson, "The Railway King" whose reputation aroused considerable unease in Hull. Perhaps this was somewhat ameliorated when Hudson engaged his architect, G. T. Andrews, to build the splendid new Paragon Station, opened in 1848, and its associated hotel.

The coming of the railway put an end to a brief and exciting period when paddle steamers competed for the expanding passenger trade between Hull and London. The first steamship on the Humber, the *Caledonia*, began plying between Hull and Selby in 1815, but by 1823 two bigger "paddlers", *Yorkshireman* and *Kingston*, were making regular sailings to London. Other vessels were soon added, competing with each other for size and speed. One of the most famous was the *Wilberforce* belonging to the Humber Union Steam Packet Co. `She was 200ft from taffrail to figurehead, and could accommodate 200 passengers. Her popularity was such that the marine artist John Ward painted her, and an engraving of his work found a ready market.

Sailings occasioned great excitement, and the *Hull Free Press* published in 1858 some memories, which were perhaps rather tongue-in-cheek: "Porters fought for the luggage of passengers, and sometimes the passengers themselves were seized. People seeking only the river steamers were directed to the London ones to swell the numbers, and rustics bound for Thorne found themselves bound for London.

"The interest was intense. The tide is up, and the piers crowded with spectators. In the roads, trim as gentlemen's yachts, are the rival steamers hung with colours. Rival bands strive to play each other down, rival porters bawl each other out of breath, and the rival steamers give voice from their brazen throats, and snort out, like impatient steeds, their challenges with all the energy of 300 horse-power".

Amid all the excitement, some very serious brass was being made, often by people who began life in poverty. An example was Thomas Thompson, known as "Salt Tom", who owned one of the first iron-hulled vessels on the Humber, the barque *Iron Gem*, built in 1846. As a boy, he had run away from a farm, vowing never to return, but in old age it pleased him to go back to the village from which he had escaped. News soon spread of the arrival of a sturdy old gentleman in a splendid carriage, who was in the process of distributing largesse, £10 as the prize in a quoits match, £10 to be given to the poor. Great was the excitement, and amid much speculation one of the elders recalled young Tom, the farm boy who had disappeared. Now he was back, rich, generous, an Alderman of Kingston-upon-Hull, and a former Mayor of that great town.

Not all speculation was successful, however. The Hull and Barnsley Railway and its associated Alexandra Dock, authorised by Act of Parliament in 1880, were very much local enterprises, backed by local money, including an investment of £100,000 by the Corporation. The line was not a financial success for its investors, but it did provide a link with the Yorkshire coalfield, and had a

The artist John Ward (1798-1849) produced this oil painting entitled "Hull from the Humber" in about 1837. The tower of Holy Trinity Church appears behind the buildings lining the waterfront, and to the left a very early paddle steamer emits a plume of smoke from its long funnel.

The picture was found by Mr J.G. Speight, the Hull Reference Librarian, who had it cleaned and restored, and sold it for £50 to the Ferens Fund in 1944, thereby ensuring that it would have a permanent home in the city's Ferens Art Gallery. Hull. This is one of the finest provincial galleries in England, and such paintings as Ward's form a very strong marine collection.

part to play in an increasingly important export trade that peaked in 1914, when 4,500,000 tons of coal went abroad from Hull.

In the latter part of the 19th Century a number of entrepreneurs exploited opportunities for trade that benefited the community as well as themselves. When Thomas Wilson died in 1867, his sons Charles and Arthur took on his business, Thomas Wilson and Co, and became the world's biggest ship-owners. Their fleet of more than 100 vessels, with green hulls and black and red funnels, sailed the world.

Charles, who assumed the leading role, was a dominant figure who combined business with a Parliamentary career as Liberal MP for Hull from 1874-1905. Arthur, too, interested himself in public affairs, and served a term as Sheriff of Hull. Their motto was "Business first, and everything else afterwards" and it was rumoured that they shared £2m profits in a single year. Charles established himself at Warter Priory, a vast Victorian mansion near Pocklington, which was eventually demolished in 1972. He was raised to the peerage as Lord Nunburnholme in 1906, the year before his death. Arthur built Tranby Croft near Anlaby, a three-storey, yellow brick house of Italianate design, and also had a house in London, 17 Grosvenor Square. This enabled his wife and his daughter Ethel to cut such a dash that it was said that fashionable ladies of the Marlborough House Set ordered their gowns from the Wilsons' dressmaker, a Madame Clapham of Hull, who

This picture dates from the 19th Century and records a triumph on the part of the great Hull engineering firm of Priestman's. It shows a small dredging crane that the company had developed, and which won orders from around the world. One of the first was acquired by a Hull dock company in 1878, and is seen here demonstrating its prowess. Could the gentlemen in straw boaters at the stern of the barge be possible customers?

Priestman's developed the world's first oil engine long before Diesel and a range of excavators, cranes and grabs. Several 19th Century Hull entrepreneurs founded famous firms that bore their names. Along with Priestman's, there were Earle's (shipbuilders), Wilson's (shipowners), Reckitt's (pharmaceuticals), Blundell's (paint). Rank's (flour millers) and Hellyer's (fishing fleet owners).

prospered wondrously, eventually employing 150 girls. Madame counted Queen Maud of Norway among her customers, and continued in business until her death in 1952 at the age of 96.

In 1890 Mr and Mrs Charles Wilson achieved what must have seemed the pinnacle of society when the Prince of Wales accepted an invitation to stay with them at Tranby Croft while in the north for the Doncaster St Leger race week. Alas for the Wilsons, on the very first night of the Prince's stay, a fellow guest, Sir William Gordon-Cumming, of the Scots Guards, was accused of cheating at cards, thus associating the Wilsons and Tranby Croft for all time with what became known as the Royal Baccarat Scandal.

This old postcard shows trawlers that were fired on during the "Russian Outrage" in the North Sea in 1904 when a Russian fleet was steaming through on its way to the Far East, where it was to tackle the Japanese navy. On 19th October Hull's Gamecock fleet of trawlers reached its fishing ground on the Dogger Bank.

They were sighted by the Tsar's warships, and the Russians somehow convinced themselves that they were in danger of attack from Japanese torpedo boats, and opened fire. The Hull men, caught in the glare of searchlights and beset by shellfire, shouted and waved their arms at their attackers. "To show what we were, I held a big plaice up," one said later, "My mate showed a haddock".

One trawler, Crane, was sunk, and others damaged. Two men were killed and others injured. The Royal Navy put itself at readiness for retaliation, and by the evening of 26th October twenty-eight battleships were either at sea or had steam up, ready to destroy the Russian squadron at a word from Whitehall.

That word did not come. The Russian Minister for Foreign Affairs, Count Lamsdorf, called at the British Embassy in Moscow with a request to pass on to King Edward VII and the British Government the Tsar's sincere regret. Somehow it all blew over, and Hull was left to bury its dead, George Smith, skipper of the Crane, and the trawler's third hand, William Leggett.

For another seaman, Edwin Costello of the trawler Gull, there was recognition in the form of the Albert Medal for his gallantry in rescuing the crew of the Crane and recovering the bodies of the men killed.

The Russian fleet duly sailed on round the world and was utterly destroyed at Tsu-Shima by a Japanese force commanded by Admiral Heihachiro Togo.

Such goings-on would have been unlikely at the home of another Hull-born industrial magnate, Joseph Arthur Rank, who was a staunch and lifelong Methodist. His father, Joseph Rank, was born in 1854 at a mill in Holderness Road owned by his grandfather. His father had a similar business in Southcoates Lane, and Joseph also became a master-miller. In 1885 he opened Alexandra Mill, the first roller-mill in Hull, employing a process for treating grain that had been pioneered in Hungary and the United States. It was successful, and only six years later he added an even bigger venture, Clarence Mill on the bank of the River Hull. By then he was among his home town's biggest employers.

Joseph Arthur Rank was born in 1888, and was still a boy when his father eventually moved to London. His initial interest in films was as a means of propagating the Gospel. Known to the public as J. Arthur Rank, he was a chairman of several film companies including Gaumont-British, and worked hard to counter Hollywood's monopoly of the industry. He was created 1st Baron Rank in 1957, and died in 1972.

Hull surged magnificently forward throughout the 19th Century, and deservedly achieved the status of a city in 1897. By then it was developing rapidly as a fishing port, and such men as Samuel Priestman and Isaac Reckitt had established businesses whose names were destined to resonate throughout the business world. The new city brandished as a symbol of its success the astonishing Dock Offices, completed in 1871 to a design by Christopher George Wray, and soon added further architectural splendours, Sir Edwin Cooper's Guildhall, and City Hall, which was designed by the first City Architect, Joseph Hirst.

Some wealthy citizens were prepared to spend money for the benefit of the community as a whole. James Reckitt provided Hull with its first public library in Holderness Road, which opened in 1889, and to which Francis Reckitt added a reference section in 1890. In 1905 Thomas Robinson Ferens gave the site for the art gallery that bears his name, and added £45,000 to pay for the building. This great benefactor (1847-1930) worked his way up from confidential shorthand clerk to the joint chairmanship of Reckitt's, and was Liberal MP for East Hull from 1906 to 1918. He was also a prime mover in establishing Hull University when, in 1925, he put up £250,000 towards the project.

Ferens was consulted in the early stages of what became a great philanthropic housing development. In 1907 Sir James Reckitt wrote to him of his plan to "establish a garden village within a reasonable distance of our Works, so that those who are wishful might have the opportunity of living in a better house, with a garden, for the same rent that they now pay". This idea very soon came to fruition on 130 acres of the Holderness House estate that Sir James bought from the Jalland family. Some 500 homes were erected in what John Markham in his *Streets of Hull* (Highgate Publications 1990) called "one of Hull's most successful pieces of town planning, with winding tree-lined roads and well-built houses, which still presents an evocative – if idealised – picture of an Edwardian village."

An elegant array of carriages awaits passengers disembarking at the Victoria Pier, Hull, after crossing the Humber. One of the curiosities of the New Holland ferry, latterly operated by the three ferries as described in the chapter 'Big Ships and Small Boats', was that tickets included payments made to Hull Corporation for the use of its Pier. When I travelled in 1968, I was told that the Corporation's share was 1d on a single ticket and 2d on a return. Cars earned the city 1s single and 2s return.

Associated Humber Lines, a British Railways subsidiary, operated the service, and the railway influence was inescapable. Passengers at the Hull end booked their tickets at a terminal that was a prime example of Victorian railway architecture, complete with a monstrous coke stove in the booking hall. Overall control was exercised by the stationmaster at mainline Paragon.

A cluttered quayside at Hull in 1964, with lorries and railway vans being loaded or unloaded.

Left-hand drive Ford Corsair saloons in orderly queues to await export from Hull docks in August 1964.

In the 1950s Marie Hartley and Joan Ingilby included Hull in their The Wonders of Yorkshire and in doing so provided an invaluable portrait of a seafaring city at its most prosperous. They listed 11 docks, from St Andrew's, where the fish was landed, to Salt End, where oil was piped ashore. Cargoes were shifted by 4,000 dockers, and as many again were employed in support roles.

In addition, Hull was the premier fishing port in Britain. Hartley and Ingilby traced its eminence back to the opening of the rail link with the West Riding in 1840, and the discovery of a cheap method of making ice. They were taken on a tour of St Andrew's Dock and wrote of their impressions:

"At the fish dock, what a scene of pushing, hurrying, shouting men and boys! On the quayside, silhouetted against the water, groups of filleters, clad in white coats, oilskin aprons, leggings, and clogs, wield knives with deft rhythmic strokes. Men roll kits, boys trundle crates.

"The trawlers sail in on the evening tide, and start unloading at 2 a.m. By 7 a.m. all is ready for the auctions. All might seem confusion, but in fact it is highly organised. The fish is loaded expeditiously into lorries or into railway wagons lined up behind each buyer's office. On an average, 1,000 tons of fish are landed daily.

"About 100 of the 142 trawlers are big modern vessels of 800 tons, manned by crews of 25 or 30 men. The skippers earn £100 a week. Some save it and become trawler owners themselves, others fritter it all away".

Neither Marie Hartley nor Joan Ingilby can possibly have imagined that before the turn of the century all would have gone, trawlers, trawlermen, filleters, St Andrew's Dock, the lot. They were the victims of the second blitz that struck Kingston-upon-Hull, an economic blitz, which destroyed or diminished many of its industries and brought a proud city to its knees.

This had never happened in Hitler's blitz, the first air-raid alert for which had sounded early on September 4, 1939, and for which the last all clear was not heard until March 20, 1945.

In the intervening five-and-a-half years, the city was bombed 80 times and 1,200 of its citizens were killed. More than 3,500 houses were demolished, and 80,000 damaged. Twenty-five schools were destroyed, and 85 damaged. All the main hospitals were hit, as were the Guildhall, the City Hall, the Ferens Art Galley, the head Post Office, and five museums.

The city's suffering was not made public. Censorship ensured that it was referred to in news bulletins only as "a town in the North East". Years later the then Bishop of Hull, the Rt Rev James Hullen, was moved to write to The Times: "The people of Hull to this day feel great anguish that the devastation of their city has never been recognised, either in Britain or in Europe.

"Nearly 10 per cent of the city's homes were either destroyed or seriously damaged, and only a few buildings were left standing in the centre of the city. As well as targeting the railway, docks and industry the warplanes would, on their return flights (from other targets), discharge their bombs indiscriminately over Hull, killing and maiming thousands of innocent civilians. This has left a mark, not just on the terrain, but on the interior landscape of people's souls."

The Bishop concluded his letter with a plea that the nation should not forget the people of Hull, now "a modern and vibrant city".

While their homes were being pounded by the Luftwaffe, Hull's servicemen and women served gallantly in the theatres of war, like the men of the Merchant Navy who took their ships through

Arctic waters on the perilous voyages to Murmansk with vital supplies for Russia.

Many perished as the result of enemy action. Others died in accidents, none more tragic than the disaster that befell members of the Humber Division Royal Naval Volunteer Reserve. They were drafted "for the duration" in August 1939, before the war had even begun, and some joined the HMS *Curacao*, a cruiser built in 1917, and known below decks as "The Cocoa Boat".

On 2nd October 1942 she had a rendezvous with the liner *Queen Mary* (81,235 tons) in mid-Atlantic to escort her home. Due to a misunderstanding during zig-zagging, the Cunard liner, with 10,000 American troops aboard, struck the 4,100-ton cruiser, slicing her in two. Only 72 of her crew of 400 survived, among them a Hull reservist, Ted Wilson.

When John Dunning produced his book *Hull Division Royal Naval Volunteer Reserve: The Men and their Ships* (Bishop Burton Books, 1995), Mr Wilson contributed a gripping chapter describing his rescue, and recalling how the survivors were marched into a hall as soon as they landed, and told that what had happened must be kept secret. So it remained until after the war.

There is an eerie footnote to this tale. A reliable informant told Mr Dunning that the sister of John Thorpe, an Able Seaman on Curacao, was in her walk-in pantry when she sensed rather than heard a movement behind her.

On turning round, she was amazed to see her brother standing in the doorway, for he was not expected home on leave. He was in uniform, and he said: "I have come to say goodbye, for I shall not be seeing you again."

Two days later, the family received a telegram informing them of his loss, and John Thorpe is commemorated on the Chatham Naval Memorial for those with no known grave. His apparition appeared during the afternoon of 2nd October 1942, which, as his family learned later, was about the time of the sinking of his ship.

As the 21st Century unfolds, there is a feeling that Hull could do with some firm leadership. Its traditional jobs have gone and its tight-knit communities, like those on Hessle Road and Beverley Road, have been scattered in new suburbs. Hull has sore need of the zeal for education of a Ferens, the entrepreneurial flair of a Reckitt, and the kind of courage that saw Sir John Hotham defy his King from the battlements.

Ironicall, the city that proffited from watersuffered by it too during the disastrous summer floods of 2007. As with the Blitz, its travails at first went virtually unoticed elsewher, especially in Westminster.

THEN AND NOW – HULL AND ITS DOCKS

Hull's range of magnificent buildings includes the Dock Offices, which is a prosaic name for a building that fairly trumpeted the wealth and power of the port. Nothing but the best went into its construction, Ancaster stone for the facing, Bramley Fell stone from Hawksworth, Leeds, for the basement, and Portland stone for the many sculptured facings. It was built in 1867-1871 by Christopher G Wray, a London-based architect whose design, crowned by triumphant triple domes, won approval against a plan drawn up by Cuthbert Brodrick, a Yorkshireman famous for Leeds Town Hall and the Grand Hotel, Scarborough. The building now provides a worthy setting for the Hull Maritime Museum. On its original site is the column bearing the statue of William Wiberforce, the anti-slave trade campaigner, which was erected in 1835.

An aerial picture of Hull shows Queen's Dock, poking like a watery finger right into the heart of the city. This shot must date from the 1920s, for the dock, opened 1778, was closed in 1930, and filled in to provide Hull with Queen's Gardens in place of the ten acres of water.

Trawler skippers aimed to land their catches in time for the lucrative Good Friday market. This picture shows part of the Eastertide harvest under scrutiny from buyers in 1954.

This photograph, taken on 4th October, 1937, shows the bustle of activity that characterised the lower reaches of the River Hull, a modest waterway that gave its name to England's eighth city and third seaport. In the basin now is berthed the Arctic Corsair, a 1960s sidewinder trawler that is a floating contribution to Hull's museum district. Nearby are the Streetlife Museum, celebrating 200 years of transport, and the East Riding Museum with its Roman mosaics. Further along High Street is Wilberforce House, the birthplace of the city's most famous son. It is now dedicated to his memory, and was refurbished for the bicentenary of the abolition of the slave trade within the British Empire, the cause to which Wilberforce devoted much of his life.

In the years immediately after the 1939-1945 war huge catches were made in seas that had been left virtually unfished for six years. This photograph from 1947 shows a lorry taking barrels of fish for processing, possibly for conversion into fishmeal, used as a fertiliser. In the railway siding in the background is a line of vans used to form fish trains. Good connections were vital to inland markets, for they carried the most perishable of foodstuffs.

This view of St Andrew's Dock at Hull dates from 1956, and shows it crowded with fishing vessels. The dock opened in 1883, dedicated solely to the use of the fishing community, and it was so successful that it was extended in 1895.

In the intervening years the trawlers had extended their range to Icelandic waters and the Faeroes. From the early 19th Century successive improvements in fishing techniques facilitated larger catches. The first steam trawler, Zodiac, entered service in 1882, signalling the eventual disappearance of the sailing smack.

More recently, stern fishing began in the 1960s. Catches were frozen so the fish could be held in store and distributed to meet the needs of the market.

Fish stocks came under pressure. The Hull fleet had abandoned the North Sea in favour of distant grounds, and it was hit hard in 1975 when Iceland extended its territorial waters from 50 to 200 miles, triggering the third "Cod War".

By the end of 1976, grounds in the Arctic, and around the Faeroes, the Norwegian coast and Newfoundland were forbidden to British fishermen. By then St Andrew's Dock had closed, because the expansion of the freezer trawler fleet had prompted a decision to move the fish docks to new buildings in Albert Dock. Work on filling in St Andrew's began in the late 1980s

Although Hull may not catch many fish nowadays, vast quantities are still imported.

Hull Fish Dock in 2002 shows clear water where once it would have been possible to cross by stepping from the deck of one vessel to the next. (Simon Hulme/YPN)

View at dawn on a January day in 2005, looking towards the British Petroleum Saltend refinery from a walkway alongside the old Victoria Dock at Hull. Here, the cooling towers, chimneys and silos rise ghost-like from the depths, but in the cold light of day the installation looks what it is – a substantial contributor to the British economy. (Terry Carrot/YPN)

This book began at the Tees estuary and finishes at the Humber estuary, both of which are spanned by magnificent bridges of very different character.

Crossing the Humber Bridge by car is a pleasant experience, but not greatly out of the ordinary. You just sweep along between the East Riding and Lincolnshire as if travelling an ordinary highway, albeit one suspended 100ft above the Humber at high water. To sense the full majesty of this spectacular piece of engineering, the visitor needs to get out of his car and use one of the viewing areas or, even better, walk beneath the bridge on its north bank, the vantage point from which this picture was taken. It was the longest suspension bridge in the world when it was opened by the Queen on 17th July 1981, and a triumph for its creators, Freeman, Fox and Partners. (Jim Moran/YPN)

The much earlier Transporter Bridge at Middlesbrough, seen here in splendid silhouette, was authorised by Act of Parliament in 1907, after a vigorous campaign by Alderman Joseph McLaughlan and the threat of a private enterprise bridge had swayed Middlesbrough Town Council. The builder was Sir William Arrol and Co of Glasgow, and the structure was opened when Prince Arthur of Connaught, a son of Queen Victoria, threw a gold switch on 17th October 1911. The bridge carries up to 600 people or eight to ten motor vehicles on a platform (known as the car) that shuttles to and fro across the Tees, suspended from the superstructure. One of only three such bridges in England, it was an immediate success, with 6,290 people crossing on the first day and 2,657,206 in the first year, during which the Council reaped a gross profit of £4,675 3s 1d. Nearly 100 years on, it is still doing its job. (Mike Cowling/YPN)

BIG SHIPS AND SMALL BOATS

The date is 28th October 1945, and the Southern Venturer, *a whaling factory ship, is being shepherded along the Humber by a gaggle of tugs that serves to emphasise the sheer size of the bigger vessel. Christian Salvesen and Co Ltd of Leith, Scotland, at that time world leaders in whale fishing by factory methods, operated the* Venturer *and her sister-ship,* Southern Harvester. *These enormous vessels took on board whales slaughtered by smaller boats, known as catchers, which worked in numbers of about ten to each "mother" ship. Their activities meant the Antarctic's stock of the great creatures that formed their prey was soon drastically reduced.* Southern Venturer *was sold to the Japanese when Salvesen's withdrew from whaling, and no doubt continued her depredation in icy waters round the South Pole.*

There can hardly be a greater contrast than that between the vast bulk of the Southern Venturer *and the delicate lines of the hull, mast and rigging of the* Harmony, *seen here in an engraving published by Yorkshire Notes and Queries in 1907, yet both were engaged in the whale fishery. However, more than a hundred years, and great sophistication of whale-slaughtering techniques, separated their activities.*

The plate from which the engraving was printed was made in 1829, and dedicated to Harmony's *owner, Thomas Bell. The ship made her first Arctic voyage from Hull in 1806, and already had an interesting history. She was built in America, and how she came to be sailing under the English flag is not certain. During and immediately prior to the American War of Independence, a number of shipowners who remained loyal to the Crown left the United Sates and registered their ships in England. Another possibility is that she was a prize seized during the war, like another Hull whaler, the* Truelove.

Harmony *fished successfully over a long number of years, and was still going to the Davis Strait as late as 1837. She was reckoned to have accounted for 216 whales and 975 seals, and became known affectionately on the Hull waterfront as "Old Harmony". The engraving shows several rowing boats pursuing whales, while seamen on the ice hunt down seals. Strips of blubber are being cut from a whale drawn up alongside* Harmony.

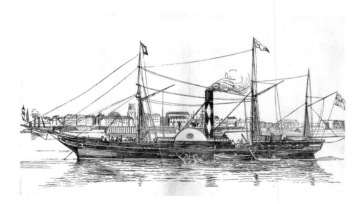

This engraving shows the Hull paddle steamer William Wilberforce, *popular with passengers on the service between the Humber and the Thames that flourished until the coming of the railways.*

A magnificent sight tied up on arrival in Hull of 23rd June 1938 is the sailing ship Passat, *at that time flying the Finnish flag. She was a four-masted steel barque built in 1911 at the Hamburg shipyard of Blohm and Voss for a German owner. In 1921, she was handed to France as compensation for war damage. Her German owner bought her back, though, and he eventually sold her to Gustav Erikson of Mariehamn, Finland, in 1932.*

Laid up during the 1939-1945 war, she was back on the high seas in 1946, and in 1947 sailed from Australia to Falmouth, Cornwall, in 143 days. She clipped that time to 109 days in 1949. She eventually returned to German ownership, and since 1960 has been anchored at Travemünde, Lübeck, where she is at the same time a showpiece and a museum. During her long career as a windjammer Passat *rounded Cape Horn 39 times, and circumnavigated the globe in 1932 and 1948.*

With the war barely over, Hull resumed its sea-going links with Germany, commercial common-sense having overcome any prejudice that might have been aroused by the Luftwaffe's success in damaging 92% of the city's houses. The Liberty ship Empire Rapier, seen here docked in Hull on 16th October 1945, was used by the Furness, Withy line on the new route to Cuxhaven on the shore of the Heligoland Bight near Hamburg, Germany. .

    The previous year she had sailed with the D-Day armada, her decks crowded with infantrymen ready to fight their way ashore on 6th June. Empire Rapier was built by Consolidated Steel at Wilmington, California, USA in 1943 for the US Maritime Commission, and sailed under British colours as a troop carrier She was scrapped at Kearney, New Jersey, USA in 1966.

The paddleboat ferry Tattershall Castle *leaves Hull for New Holland on the Lincolnshire shore in February 1948. With her sister ship, the* Wingfield Castle, *she had come into service in 1934, both having been built by William Gray and Co of Hartlepool.*

Ferries have plied the Humber estuary since Roman and Anglo-Saxon times, and Humber keels, driven by sail, maintained the service well into the 19th Century. The paddler Caledonia *inaugurated the first steam ferry service in 1814. The shortest and possibly the most profitable route across the Humber was between Hull and New Holland, and in the late 1820s this was being operated by a small wooden paddle steamer,* Magna Carta.

Tattershall Castle, Wingfield Castle *and a third similar vessel,* Lincoln Castle, *built in 1940, were owned by the London and North Eastern Railway Company (LNER) and passed to British Railways on nationalisation. Between them, the boats were carrying 1,000.000 passengers, along with flocks of sheep up to 200 strong, horses, and gipsies with their caravans on their way to Hull Fair. I made a crossing in 1968 and wrote in the* Yorkshire Post *that the three paddlers were "really the last refugees of the steam age so far as British Railways in concerned. Powered by engines that gobble through as much as seven tons of coal a day, they recall a grimier and more gracious age of transport."*

Soon, however, the Humber was to be bridged. Tattershall Castle *was sold in 1972 and became a floating restaurant on the Victoria Embankment in London. In 1974, at 5.31 pm on 14th March* Wingfield Castle *made her last departure from the Victoria Pier, Hull. At the helm was Capt Stan Wright, her skipper for 18 years. She is now back among other historic ships at Hartlepool, restored and preserved.*

In 1968 I wrote in the Yorkshire Post*: "But the most evocative of the palmy days of the LNER is the smell. It is that half-remembered heady perfume that recalls catching the mail train on a foggy morning. It is at its most intense in the gangway on* Lincoln Castle *from which it is possible to watch the stoker feeding his boilers, and the rods of the triple-expansion engine wheezing bravely back and forth."*

Ferries across the Humber became redundant with the opening of the long anticipated road bridge upstream of Hull in 1981. Lincoln Castle, *like her sisters, is preserved and, beautifully restored, lying in the Alexandra Dock at Grimsby.*

BAT INTO HELL – THE HELL OF WAR

FOR many years visitors from Hull found an old friend at Bridlington ready to take them on a trip. The pleasure boat *Yorkshireman*, spent the winter months in a more workaday role, that of a Humber tug.

Yorkshireman arrived at the holiday resort fresh from Earle's Shipbuilding and Engineering Company's yard on the Humber in May 1928. She was a replacement for the old paddle-steamer *Frenchman*, built at South Shields in 1892, and owned, like *Yorkshireman*, by the United Towing Co of Hull, which was formed in 1920 by the amalgamation of seven tug companies.

Frenchman, *a paddle-powered Hull tug that also served as a pleasure boat at Bridlington.*

Yorkshireman *took over from* Frenchman.

A happy crowd of trippers aboard Yorkshireman *includes a parson who probably felt the heat in his dog collar.*

Thomas Clarkson Spink was appointed managing director, a post he held for 40 years, and it was said he liked to have one of the company's vessels at Bridlington because he had a home there.

Apart from wartime, when she was requisitioned, *Yorkshireman* spent her summers at the resort until 1954. She was certainly no ordinary tug, for her main saloon was panelled in polished mahogany, and there was a a ladies' saloon aft. She soon became a great favourite, capable of taking up to 400 holidaymakers at a time on her regular sailings. Her last trip under her own steam, before she was towed across the North Sea to shipbreakers in Belgium, was under the command of Walter Richardson.

He recalled later that he had been aboard only once before. He was visiting Bridlington with his wife Dorothy when a work colleague hailed him from the deck of *Yorkshireman*. "Fancy a trip, Walt?" he called, and that was how a Hull tugmaster spent part of his holiday going to sea in a Hull tug.

The Hull tug Brahman, *renamed* Bat *during the war.*

Walt's father was James Richardson, one of the salty characters of the Hull waterfront. He spent a lifetime on the tugs, and in 1939 took one of them to war. She was the *Brahman*, 230 tons, built by Cochrane's of Selby in 1938, and requisitioned by the Admiralty within a month of the outbreak of the 1939-1945 war.

The Navy changed her name to *Bat*, not wishing the little Hull tug to be confused with the battleship *HMS Barham*, destined to be lost with 862 of her crew in the Mediterranean in November 1942. *Bat* took part in two great Naval occasions during the war. The first was the rescue of the destroyer *HMS Kelly*, commanded by Lord Louis Mountbatten (later Earl Mountbatten of Burma, victim of a cowardly murder by the IRA).

While leading a flotilla in a North Sea sweep, *Kelly* was struck by a torpedo from a German E-

Boat, which blasted a 50ft long hole in her side, killing or injuring scores of her crew. She was at first taken in tow by another destroyer, *HMS Bulldog*, but the next day, with *Kelly* wallowing in the water, *Bat* took up the line.

There was an immediate understanding between Lord Louis, who refused to leave his post for 90 hours, and Jim Richardson, who stood unflinchingly on his open bridge despite Luftwaffe sorties. Eventually, they shared a triumph, and were cheered by excited crowds as *Kelly* berthed in the Tyne. Lord Louis ensured that the tug's skipper's skill was recognised and Jim Richardson was appointed MBE.

Later, he was Mentioned in Despatches for his part in another perilous enterprise, the assembly of Mulberry Harbours off the Normandy coast that began on D-Day, 6th June 1944.

James Richardson
– a lifetime in tugs.

James Richardson was one of those stockily-built men who sometimes seem as broad as they are long. His face on old photographs brings the British Bulldog irresistibly to mind. He did not swear, a rarity among tugmen, and neither did he drink, rarer still. He could perhaps be described as a pragmatic teetotaller though. In the days before the general adoption of wireless telegraphy, when tugs tied up at Paull jetties ready to greet incoming merchantmen with offers of help, he and his wife ran the Crown Inn in the village, and Jim was sure of a good trade among his fellow rivermen.

He died in 1962, the year after *Brahman* was sold out of Hull. To the end he treasured a flimsy transcript of a signal: "Goodbye *Bat* and all the best. You have done splendid work here, and we are proud to have known and worked with you."

It was a personal message as he steamed home from the war, and it came from Admiral Sir Henry Harwood, hero of the Battle of the River Plate in which the German pocket battleship *Graf Spee* was destroyed, who ended the war as Flag Officer Commanding Orkney and Shetland.

Walter Richardson was the third of James Richardson's five sons. When he left school during the war, his father found him a shore job at Reckitt's. But Walter was having none of that. He shipped on a merchantman, *Empire Newton*, that was ferrying supplies to the Normandy beachheads, and on his first voyage as a sixteen year old, his ship was bombed, shelled and machine-gunned.

He reached the Mulberry at Arromanches, and amid the clamour of war found his father on the deck of *Bat* with a bucket at his feet, calmly dhobying his clothes. "Hello, Dad, " said Walt, whereupon his father nearly fell in the bucket.

After the war, Walt went big-boating, as they say in Hull, and sailed twice round the world on tramp steamers. But in 1950 he married my wife's cousin, Dorothy, who provided him with four beautiful daughters, and it was back to the river for Walt. He became one of the Humber's most experienced tugmasters, and among his early commands was *Krooman*, sister-ship to his father's famous *Brahman*. "I was so proud," said Walt, "she might have been *Queen Mary*."

SIR HENRY'S AMAZING SEA-SICKNESS CURE

DURING a voyage from Calais to Dover in 1868, Henry Bessemer suffered grievously from seasickness. He was an inventor, responsible for successful innovations including a cheap process of making steel, which bore his name and made his fortune and that of many others, including that of Andrew Carnegie, the American magnate.

The illness persisted when he returned to London, and was so acute that a doctor sat at his bedside all night. Eventually he was dosed with prussic acid, which may sound rather drastic, but afterwards he began to feel better.

It was this bout of *mal de mer* that turned his mind to another invention, and he set about devising a vessel capable of carrying passengers through severe weather in a state of equilibrium – a wonder of the sea that became known as the Ship with the Swinging Saloon.

At that time, when Bessemer had an idea, people listened. He was a self-taught genius, and his inventions worked, and made money, lots of money. He perfected a process for using brass powder in place of gold in paint-making, a method he kept secret for 30 years, thus ensuring himself another fortune. He produced embossed stamps for title deeds, suggested cancelling postage stamps by printing the date on them, turned graphite dust into pencils, and answered a challenge from Prince Albert by putting together a hydraulic device for the extraction of juice from sugar cane.

These and other wonders cascaded from him; wealth and honours cascaded on him. He was knighted by Queen Victoria in 1879, made a member of the Royal Society, and in the USA the steel manufacturer Henry Fairfield DeBardeleben named a city after him. Bessemer, Alabama, now has a population of nearly 30,000.

It was hardly surprising, therefore, that Henry Bessemer quickly attracted investors when he came up with a new scheme, even one as outlandish as making ships proof against causing seasickness. That is probably why a Hull firm, Earle's Shipbuilding and Engineering Co Ltd, became involved.

A heavyweight in the business of designing ships, Edward James Reed, who had been chief constructor for the Royal Navy from 1863 to 1870, was closely associated with the Hull company, and became naval constructor to the Bessemer Saloon Ship Company.

A director of Earle's, Admiral Sir Robert Spencer Robinson, also joined the Saloon Ship board, and the contract to build *SS Bessemer* duly went to the Hull yard that had been established by two brothers, Charles and William Earle, in 1845.

They had never before produced such a weird craft. She had a bow at each end so she might go in and out of narrow harbours, like that at Calais, without turning round. She had two funnels, two pairs of paddle wheels, two engines, and two rudders. She was 350ft long and 50ft wide, and her twin prows were set low in the water. Designer Reed said this "low freeboard at the extremities"

Sir Henry Bessemer

was a suggestion from Bessemer, and was supposed to reduce pitching.

The centrepiece of this bizarre creation was suspended amidships, a luxurious passenger saloon 70 feet long and 30 feet wide, hung on longitudinal pivots and controlled by hydraulic machinery.

The idea was that when the ship rolled, the saloon would be moved in the opposite direction, thus keeping it upright. Even in the roughest seas, passengers would not be inconvenienced. Seasickness would be a discomfort of the past – that at least was the idea. In practice, the saloon did not work, or (as Bessemer asserted in his autobiography) was never given a chance to work.

A demonstration of the *SS Bessemer* was arranged for 8th May, 1875. The Saloon Ship Company decided it would be prudent to have a discreet trial beforehand.

Captain Pittock, an able steamboat commander with 20 years' experience of sailing into Calais harbour in all weathers, took charge. Yet on a calm morning, he was unable to keep *Bessemer* off the Calais pier, which she hit with a paddle wheel, causing much damage.

Bessemer was repaired in time for 8th May, but so much work had been necessary that there was no opportunity for Bessemer to bring his work on the saloon to completion and test it at sea. Unwilling to give his invention a first trial on a public occasion, he fixed it rigidly in place, so the voyage was not a test of the saloon, but of *Bessemer*. She failed, She was slow, and she handled badly, and Bessemer told the rest of the story in his autobiography, published seven years after his death in 1898:

"We had arrived – very slowly I admit – at the entrance to Calais harbour. I, knowing what had occurred on a previous occasion, held my breath while the veteran Captain Pittock gave his orders to the man at the helm. But the ship did not obey him and crash she went along the pier side, knocking down huge timbers like so many ninepins. I knew what it all meant to me. That five minutes had made me a poorer man by £34,000 (his investment in the Saloon Company) and it had deprived me of one of the greatest triumphs of a long professional life."

Subsequently there was much laying of blame. Bessemer complained that Reed's ship could neither steam rapidly not steer safely. Andrew Betts Brown, the patentee of the hydraulic gear used aboard, also blamed Reed's design. Reed blamed Brown's gear. Both Reed and Brown blamed Bessemer. Admiral Sir Robert Spencer Robinson reported to fellow directors of the Bessemer Steamboat Saloon Company in blunt nautical terms: "Mr Bessemer has not worked the Saloon with any successful results, and it does not seem at all possible that he will do so".

Thus daunted, the company went into liquidation, and the accommodation amidships was removed, never having swung, or not swung, as the case might have been.

I first came upon the story of the *Bessemer* in 1963. Mention of her in the *Yorkshire Evening Post* prompted a call from the Holbeck, Leeds, headquarters of William Sugden and Co. They had an archive relating to her, and it transpired that after her unsuccessful foray into the English Channel she was bought for £20,000 by William Sugden, the son of the owner of the company.

There was some suggestion in the family that he had taken it in payment of a debt. Whatever the reason for his purchase, he soon had cause to regret it. On her first trip from Hull, *Bessemer* ran aground. She was then in collision with *SS Zebra*. Blundering back into the Humber, she was stranded again. The captain wrote to Mr Sugden that he had reported the resulting damage to the agent at Hull, adding plaintively: "He seemed much surprised."

Mr Sugden, perhaps, was also surprised. He made immediate attempts to get rid of *Bessemer*. Edward Reed warned him it would be necessary to sell the ship as a great bargain. One potential buyer did offer £45,000, but only on condition that she was first cut in two amidships, and that each portion was fitted with a stern, thus giving him two ships for the price of one, the *Besse* perhaps, and the *Mer*.

The Holbeck records did not reveal the eventual fate of the *Bessemer*. The last document, appropriately a bill, was dated 1878. Mr Sugden had either sold her or decided to forget all about her. According to John Guthrie's *Bizarre Ships of the Nineteenth Century* (Hutchinson 1970) she was fitted with a conventional poop and forecastle, but at the start of a new career as a cargo carrier she was stranded on the East Coast and became a total loss, finally being broken up in 1880.

The saloon was removed, and went to Edward Reed's country home at Swanley in Kent, where it was used as a summer pavilion. Later it was used as an assembly hall at the Kent Farm and Horticultural Institute, but it was damaged during an air raid in the 1939-45 war and subsequently offered to the National Maritime Museum at Greenwich. The museum was not particularly interested, and in 1963 the Institute said it thought that the Swinging Saloon might have gone to America. It would have been shipped, of course, but it is a safe bet nobody travelled in it.

Earle's went into voluntary liquidation in the 1890s, and was acquired by Charles Wilson of the

SS Bessemer

Wilson Line, the yard's main customer. It closed in 1932, having launched nearly 700 ships between 1853 and 1931.

Reed, the designer, was granted a testimonial by the city of Hull in January 1894, before *Bessemer's* maiden voyage, and later the same year was elected MP for Pembroke in Wales. He continued to work in ship design, and in 1880 he, too, was knighted by Queen Victoria.

Sir Henry Bessemer remained unabashed to the end. He concluded his chapter on the *Bessemer* by asserting: "My hydraulic controlling apparatus was never completed, never tested at sea, and consequently never failed".

LAND FIT
FOR HEROES

AFTER the First World War, the city of Kingston-upon-Hull sought to provide Land Fit for Heroes. The site chosen was at Dunswell, a hamlet on the road to Beverley that had once been called Beerhouses in recognition of the number of inns competing to slake the prodigious thirsts of boatmen on the nearby River Hull.

But, to judge from its name, there was one teetotal outpost in this place flowing with hops and money, Sober Hall Farm of 96 acres, which, soon after the Armistice in 1918, the city bought for £10,400. To this was added the adjoining Low Cottage Farm, providing 171 acres in all. Hull County Borough Council, as it was then, was acting under the provisions of Smallholdings and Allotments Acts, the latest of which was passed in 1919, and looked to the Ministry of Agriculture and Fisheries for subsidies.

According to a return from Hull to the Ministry in November 1921, the cost of the scheme was estimated at £31,172, which would provide 22 holdings, each with its own dwelling. There would be 18 "cottage holdings" of about an acre each, and four larger ones, each of up to 41 acres. The council specified that they were for disabled ex-servicemen, and by late 1922 the tenancies were being taken up.

I wrote about this enterprise in 1996 for a Saturday column I was contributing to the *Yorkshire Post*, and, as often happened, there was a good feedback from readers.

Once letter was from Mrs Madge Silverwood, the eldest daughter of Charles E Temperton, and when we met at her flat in Pollard Court, Eldon Hall, Hull, an extraordinary story emerged. Her father took on the challenge of running a smallholding despite a cruel disablement. The war had left him blind, and as he was unable to resume his pre-war trade as a painter and decorator, St Dunstan's trained him for poultry-keeping.

He had married in 1917, and he and his wife Lily eventually had a family of five children. Charles Temperton worked hard to supplement his disability pension, and succeeded admirably according to Mrs Silverwood. "There was always a square meal on the table and a fire in the hearth," she told me, "and we were well shod and clothed." As the children grew older they were able to help in the business. Mrs Silverwood recalled guiding her father to his customers, one of his hands resting on her shoulder, the other carrying a large basket of new-laid eggs as she led him along the busy streets.

He liked to be able to do things. St Dunstan's taught him to type, and his daughter said he was good at it, making few mistakes in orders for poultry food, and letters to friends. He also mastered Braille, and had a Braille typewriter. "He was a charming and loveable man, " said Mrs Silverwood, "and he would turn his hand to anything, whether mending punctures or baking bread." He made light of his disability as, for instance, when, introduced to someone called Seymour, he joked: "If you are see-more, I am see-less."

St Dunstan's provided him with another skill, making coconut mats from coir. He worked on them in a hut on his land, and some went to Cunard for their luxury liner, *Queen Mary*.

Mrs Silverwood said that the semi-detached houses at Dunswell had no electricity or running water to begin with, and their tenants had to rely on an outside pump and oil lamps, but it was a happy community.

During the Second World War, at the suggestion of St Dunstan's, the family moved to Masongill, near Ingleton in the Yorkshire Dales, to avoid the Hull blitz. Again Mr Temperton did his bit, making camouflage nets. He was remembered with affection there, and one *Yorkshire Post* reader, who had made friends with the family, called Mr Temperton "one of the most remarkable men I have ever known, with a wicked sense of humour.

"In summer he would sit out of doors in a deckchair to shave himself. One day, he sat down with his kit, then said to me: 'Damn, I forgot the mirror, please go and ask Mrs Temperton for it'. I did, whereupon she turned to me and asked what on earth he would do with it. The penny dropped!

"When I last saw him, after a break of nine or ten years, he recognised my voice instantly. I often think of him."

Charles and Lily eventually moved back to Hull, where they both died aged 86, having celebrated their Diamond Wedding.

Another ex-serviceman who prospered at Dunswell was George Southwick, who took on one of the larger holdings and kept cows. He launched Southwick's Whole Dairies in Ryde Street, Hull. This business became a founder of Northern Dairies.

A friend of George Southwick's, Arthur Leonard Barnett, who had had a milk round before the war, also took a holding. His daughter, Mrs Rita Pegg, of Swanland, Hull, who was born in 1926, said her father used to tell horrifying stories of life in Flanders with the Royal Artillery. He came home with wounds to the body and leg, and, like George Southwick, had also been gassed.

He developed a notable dairy herd, and the quality of his milk was recognised when he won a gold medal in a Yorkshire competition organised by the National Farmers' Union. In 1933 he bought Eastfield, a farm of some 50 acres at Arram, near Beverley, which he worked until his health failed prior to his death in 1954.

Most, if not all, the smallholdings are back in private hands, as is Sober Hall itself, splendidly restored by its owners Mr and Mrs Alex Mathers. In its time, Hull's version of Land Fit for Heroes served some brave men well.

GOOLE AND THE TOM PUDDINGS

SOME may quibble at the inclusion of Goole in a book about the Yorkshire coast, to which I would reply that it is a seaport, albeit 50 miles inland, and anyway its inclusion offers an excellent excuse for writing about Tom Puddings. These are the humble vessels, resembling over-sized bread tins, which were towed along Yorkshire's waterways with cargoes of coal.

Their name is intriguing, and according to the Oxford English Dictionary it was originally applied by countryfolk, for what reason remains a mystery, to a stocky waterfowl, the Little Grebe. Some unsung genius, observing the progress of the coal barges through the water, must have been reminded of the bobbing motion of the Little Grebe, and named them accordingly It was a term so apt that it won universal acceptance.

The development and exploitation of these craft was explained in detail in 1987. This was thanks to a triumvirate consisting of Mr Peter L Smith, the Wakefield Historical Society and Wakefield Metropolitan District Council. The last two, combining as Wakefield Historical Publications, brought out Mr Smith's *The Aire and Calder Navigation*, a learned work that quite properly devoted itself extensively to Tom Puddings.

They did not evolve; somebody actually sat down and invented them. He was William H. Bartholemew who, in 1852, aged only 21, had been appointed to succeed his father as engineer to the Aire and Calder Navigation company. This concern had an important role in Yorkshire's industrial development.

The lower Aire was navigable as far as Knottingley in medieval times, and construction work authorised by Act of Parliament in 1699 enabled sailings to Leeds, on the Aire, and to Wakefield, on its tributary, the Calder. A great trade soon developed, and the Navigation company sought improvements. In 1788 this led to the difficult lower reaches of the Aire being bypassed by a new canal that reached the Ouse at Selby, which thereupon became Yorkshire's principal inland port.

When the 1820s began, Goole was a muddy hamlet on low-lying land where the Ouse received water drained by the Dutch River. As its name indicates, this man-made waterway was part of the plan conceived by an engineer from Holland, Sir Cornelius Vermuyden, to drain Royal Hatfield Chase, thereby creating 70,000 acres of farmland.

Before his death in 1821, the famous engineer John Rennie had drawn up a plan for a canal from the Aire at Knottingley that would extend for 17 miles to join the Ouse, its lower length running parallel to Dutch River. George Leather of Leeds put the work in hand, and on 26th July, 1826 there came the official opening, when a small flotilla of flyboats traversed the length of the

A string of Tom Puddings obediently bobbing along in the wake of a tug in 1934.

new waterway to Goole, where they were greeted by a 21-gun salute.

This also sounded the death-knell of Selby as a principal port, for Goole, 16 miles down-river of its rival, quickly became "a monument to the high noon of the canal age", according to Baron F. Duckham in his *The Yorkshire Ouse* (David and Charles, 1967). A company town, it was built on Navigation-owned land by the partnership of W.J. Jolliffe and Sir Edward Banks, the nation's leading civil engineering contractors, who were responsible for many projects, including bridges, lighthouses, dockyards and prisons. Sir Edward, who had begun working life as an illiterate farmhand, was in Goole for the canal opening when, according to the *Morning Chronicle*, "a large party sat down to dinner at the Banks' Arms, a magnificent hotel erected there by Sir Edward Banks".

The town grew, reaching a population of 3,629 at the 1841 census, and the waterway prospered, with increasing quantities of coal coming down from the West Riding to be transferred to coasting vessels. The Navigation's directors, however, led by the astute and diligent chairman, William Aldam of Frickley Hall, Doncaster, were increasingly concerned about the challenge posed by the railways, which penetrated their heartland when the Lancashire and Yorkshire Railway reached Goole in 1848.

A furious commercial battle raged, and freight rates were slashed. The situation became so serious that some directors of the Navigation contemplated selling or leasing the undertaking to its formidable rivals, the Lancashire and Yorkshire and North Eastern Railway companies.

This was where William Bartholomew and the Tom Puddings came in. The Navigation needed to offer a cheaper and equally expeditious means of transport if it was to compete successfully for coal traffic. Some canals were already using compartment boats towed by horses, and this gave Bartholomew inspiration. If steam power was the secret of success on the railways, why not use it on the canals? He continued with his lateral thinking, and happily hit on hoists. What they needed, he decided, was a means of lifting the compartment boats out of the water bodily, and emptying their contents into the holds of sea-going ships

In December 1861 the Navigation's directors accepted his plan. Coal would be moved in compartment boats made of iron plates, each of 25 tons capacity. They would be hauled, six at a time, by steam tugs. At Goole they would be lifted from the water by a hydraulic hoist devised by Bartholomew, and emptied by tipping, thereby eliminating the labour-intensive business of shovelling out cargoes by hand.

By September 1863 a hoist at Goole, built to Bartholomew's design, was in place. That same month the first two compartment boats were test-loaded. Once launched, the system progressed rapidly. Soon barges capable of carrying 35 tons of coal were in use, and as many as 17 to 20 were being towed by a single tug. The amount of coal carried to Goole increased rapidly, reaching half a million tons in 1875 and a million tons in 1890. The all-time record came in 1913, the *anno mirabilis* of the Tom Pudding, when 2,860,315 tons passed through the port, mostly arriving by compartment boat, more than 1,000 of which were in use on the waterways.

They were a commonplace sight. Attached in long lines to a tug, they bobbled along behind a Jebus, or false bow, that diverted turbulence created by the tug's propeller. Some were loaded by being taken from the water, mounted on bogies, and hauled direct to the pithead.

This picture, taken in May 1950, underlines the importance of Continental traffic to the port of Goole. Diana V, *leaving West Dock, was registered in The Netherlands. The arrival was* Annie Tramm, *registered in Hamburg, Germany. Work began on the West Dock in 1910, and it was in use within a year, this being the last scheme undertaken by Mr W.H. Bartholomew, who had been appointed Chief Engineer and General Manager of the Aire and Calder Navigation in 1872. He died aged 88 in 1919, having retired on a pension as a director of the Navigation, and is buried in St Peter's churchyard, Stanley, Wakefield, near his childhood home and the canal to which he had devoted his life.*

William Bartholomew was duly rewarded. He received a Royalty from all the coal transported by Tom Puddings, and in 1872 he was appointed chief engineer and general manager of the Navigation. Later he became a director, and on his death the company placed on record its "deep appreciation of the unique services tendered by him to the Navigation for 66 years". He served as chairman of the Goole Steam Shipping Company, in which the Aire and Calder company held shares, and under his control it not only paid juicy dividends of 20 per cent, but also went in for fast and efficient vessels known as "Greyhounds of the Humber".

His Tom Puddings comfortably outlasted his Greyhounds. They carried more than 128,000 tons of coal in 1980, and it was not until 1986 that the decision was taken to cease using the fleet for moving bulk cargo.

Their contribution to the success of Goole, the only seaport in the West Riding, was considerable. In the years immediately before the First World War it was ranked twelfth port in the United Kingdom. In 1905, the Yorkshire and Lancashire Railway Co used it as a base for steamship

An aerial view of Goole in September 1958. Two waterways extend into the far distance across the flat landscape. On the left is Dutch River, which was cut to speed water from the Don into the Ouse. This was an element of Sir Cornelius Vermuyden's plan to win valuable farmland by draining Hatfield Chase, an old Royal hunting forest. He was born in Zeeland, Holland, hence the waterway's name. To the right is John Rennie's canal linking Goole with the Aire at Knottingley. Rennie died before his design was put into effect, but George Leather proved a worthy successor, completing the waterway by 1825, and drawing up plans for the new port of Goole.

services with the Continent, and by 1912 had twenty-five vessels engaged on its routes.

Inevitably, Goole's docks, with their three miles of quays, dominate the town. Nikolaus Pevsner in his West Riding volume of the *Buildings of England* series found little of interest, apart from the church of St John, built by the Aire and Calder Navigation in the 1840s. This he thought remarkably large and stately, and its proximity to the docks caused him to remark that "the ecclesiastical and the nautical rarely meet so intimately".

The Banks' Hotel still stands, designated "a building of special historic interest" under the 1962 Town and Country Planning Act. Its name was changed to the Lowther Hotel, commemorating Sir John Lowther, the chairman of the Navigation at the time of the canal's opening. Goole is enjoying something of a revival in the early years of the 21st Century, with the port attracting traffic levels not seen since the 1960s. It is operated by Associated British Ports, and among significant investments were new gates for the Ocean and Victoria Docks. Sadly, the town can no longer claim to be the only seaport in the West Riding. Since 1st April, 1996, it has been part of the East Riding of Yorkshire, after suggestions that it should be tacked on to Doncaster (West Yorkshire) or Selby (North Yorkshire) had been rejected.

CLINGING TO THE EDGE – A LAND OF SHIFTING SAND

The southernmost tip of Yorkshire, Spurn Point, is a transient creation of sea currents, wind and tide, thought to have a natural lifespan of 250 years. Left to its own devices, it would grow in that time to about its present size, swelled by the southward drift of tides and currents bringing pebbles, mud and sand from the crumbling Holderness shore.

Steadily it would stretch across the Humber estuary, but then, in a great storm, the sea would crash through the narrow isthmus, creating a breach. The portion detached from the shore would form an island, and it was on just such transient land that the lost town of Ravenser Odd developed, beginning with one man living in an upturned boat, and reaching, at its apogee, the status of a borough, that returned two representatives to Parliament, and rivalled Hull for wealth and trade.

Eventually the island would be swept away, and any habitations would go too. This was the fate of Ravenser Odd in the 1340s, a disaster that greatly inconvenienced the Abbot of Meaux The town was worth £50 a year in tithes and offerings to his Abbey, which also forfeited to the sea 24 houses, a church dedicated to St Mary, and even the bodies in the graveyard, freed from their resting place by the waves.

The Abbot lamented that Ravenser Odd had provoked the wrath of God (referred to in these secular days as climate change) by wicked works, and piracies. Thus he fell into the error of believing that mankind could somehow influence such phenomena as global warming, a delusion common to this day.

Until quite recently, Spurn Point, now about three-and-a-half-miles in length, has not been allowed to proceed with its natural round of disappearance and regeneration. For 150 years or so, efforts were made to stabilise the shifting promontory, and breaches that might have presaged a further brief life as an island were sealed at the cost of great effort and expense.

This stability was considered desirable because the Point was of military importance, providing a lookout and a site from which heavy guns could protect the Humber mouth in time of war. The Ministry of Defence acquired the land from the Constable family in the early 20th Century, and held on to it until the 1960s, when it was acquired by the Yorkshire Wildlife Trust, which is now allowing nature to take its course, creating the prospect of a breach in the not too distant future.

Relics remain of the standard gauge military railway that ran its length, and of the concrete artillery and searchlight emplacements. Two miles off shore stands the Bull Sand fort, built during the First World War to command the approaches to the estuary.

Spurn is also the site of a Royal National Lifeboat Institution station, the only one in the country with a full professional crew. The seven men and their families live on site, remote from other communities.

Until the coming of the railway (a single line three-and-three-quarters of a mile in length connecting a jetty at the Head with the nearest village of Kilnsea) the only way to get to the end of

The military railway line at Spurn Point was laid down during the First World War to provide a connection between a jetty at the point where ships landed provisions and Kilnsea village. In the foreground is one of the passenger railcars. which was built specifically for the railway by Hudswell Clarke and Co Ltd of Leeds. It cost £900 and was delivered in August 1933. The twenty-seater body was made by the Leeds coachbuilders, Charles Roe and Co Ltd.

the peninsular was by boat or on foot, a weary trudge over the dunes or along the beach at low tide. The track was laid hastily during the First World War, and the service operated by steam locomotives.

The lifeboatmen had permission to use a sail bogie when no trains were scheduled. Also, in the early days, Army officers used a weird contraption, an Impala motorcar of pre-1914 vintage that had been converted to run on rails

Spurn Point acquired a place in English history in the summer of 1399, when the Duke of Lancaster landed with a small force of men-at-arms. He was welcomed by one Matthew Danthorpe, the Hermit of Spurn, who had built a small chapel there.

Being blown along the Kilnsea-Spurn railway must have been an exhilarating experience, and the passengers on the sail bogie seem to be relishing the prospect of adventure.

Later, when Richard II had been deposed, and the Duke reigned in his stead as Henry IV, he remembered the man who welcomed him on the desolate shore, and sent Matthew Danthorpe a document authorizing him to complete his chapel and hermitage, and giving him full rights over the sands and seas for two leagues around.

Richard Reedbarrow succeeded as Hermit of Spurn, and laid a petition before Parliament in the time of Henry VI, Henry IV's grandson, who had acceded to the throne in 1422. Reedbarrow sought Letters Patent enabling him to finance a beacon at Spurn Point by charging a toll on passing vessels. In support, he described how:

> *"oft-tymes, by mysadventure, many divers vessels and men,*
> *godes and marchaundises, be lost and perished, as well as by*
> *Day as by Night, for defaute of a Bekyn that shuld teche the*
> *people to hold in the right chanell".*

He won his plea, and some kind of beacon may have welcomed Edward IV when, in 1471, he landed from exile in Flanders, intent on reclaiming the throne for the Yorkist faction. This he achieved with the defeat of Warwick "The Kingmaker" at Barnet, and he continued on the throne until his death in 1483.

The subsequent history of lights on Spurn is complex. For many years, lighthouses were regarded not only as services provided for the well-being of mariners, but also as commercial enterprises yielding a handy profit for speculators. The argument was that the devotion to public good represented by spending money on beacons was suitably rewarded by any surplus the dues might provide.

The consequences of this philosophy were two-fold. At sea, mariners blundered in the dark. On land, the competing interests involved in the provision of lighthouses blundered among the shoal of

Dated 28th October 1985, this shows the famous Humber lifeboat coxswain Brian Bevan giving what the photographer described in his caption as a "last shine" to the equipment in the Spurn lighthouse. It was probably an event staged by the photographer, because polishing glass seems unlikely to have been a regular task for Mr Bevan. Four crewmen have climbed the lighthouse to watch, Peter Thorpe, Dave Cape. Syd Rollinson and Dave Bailey. Shortly afterwards, the lighthouse shone its last warning, a flash every 15 seconds visible over a distance of 17 miles.

Two views of a Humber lightship date from 1947. Since 1836, London Trinity House has been the ruling authority on all lighthouses, light vessels, buoys and beacons. Four years earlier, Hull Trinity House had placed a floating light on Bull Sand at the Humber mouth, and agreed to find £600 a year for crews' wages and the whale oil that fuelled the beacon. In 1861, this lightship was chosen by Admiral Fitzroy, the pioneer of weather forecasting, to act as a storm warning station, and equipped with cones and a drum that were hoisted to warn of forthcoming severe weather.

In the 1860s, the Hull Brethren took part in a social experiment, agreeing to take two 14-year-old lads from Castle Howard reformatory and employ them as cabin boys on the lightships. The lads' former place of residence was not to be disclosed to the other crew members, and the boys themselves were to keep it secret, too.

lawsuits, on the lee shore of Royal favour, among the fanged rocks of bankruptcy, and the submerged wrecks of claim and counter-claim

Such goings-on bedevilled Spurn, and, in the late 17th Century, a failed London haberdasher called Justinian Angell hit on the idea of rebuilding his fortunes by providing lights there and profiting from the charges he would then be able to levy on shipping. His family had received a grant of land at Spurn from James I in 1609 in return for loans to the Crown.

The likelihood is that the ground that was the subject of this grant was below low watermark by the time Justinian Angell came on the scene nearly 70 year later, but he was in no way deterred, and set up two beacons. By 1674 his high and low lights, provided by coal fires in iron cradles, were burning bravely.

He died in 1680, and his son John inherited the lights, and forthwith became involved in one of the many extraordinary chapters in the history of Spurn, for his father had quickly come into conflict with the Constable family, great magnates of the East Riding and holders of the Seigniory, or Lordship, of Holderness. Sir Henry Constable was created first Viscount Dunbar in 1620, and he and his successors claimed the land on which Angell's beacons stood. In 1686, after legal proceedings of mind-shaking complexity, which are traced with the utmost diligence in Geoffrey de Boer's *History of the Spurn Lighthouses* (1968), the Dunbar faction took direct action.

The lights' under-keeper, Robert Jackson, saw the Viscount's servants advancing under arms, and, having used a handy boat-anchor to wedge the door, took himself upstairs. But Dunbar's men, with "iron gavelocks, crowes, axes, swords and pistols", forced entry, and Jackson, was deposited as a prisoner in York Castle. Subsequently, after another bout of legal wrangling, John Angell resumed control.

Hull Trinity House, having proposed a lighthouse on Spurn in 1590, turned against the idea. In 1632, they called lights there "unusefull and needless", and in 1657 "an inconvenience and a mischief". There came a change of mind, however, when the lights of the Angell family, which had originally been at the tip of Spurn, were left behind as the spit extended a further mile into the estuary, and became dangerously misleading.

The Brethren campaigned for their replacement, but needed two Acts of Parliament to overcome the objections of the Angell family, who had presumably recaptured their possessions following the war-like incursion of the Dunbar faction. Eventually Trinity House had its way, and by 1776 two stone towers had been erected by the Yorkshire civil engineer John Smeaton.

They came under the control of London Trinity House in 1836, when an Act of Parliament vested it with control of all lighthouses.

Smeaton's towers were replaced in 1895 when a new lighthouse was erected to the design of Thomas Matthews. It is now an empty shell, having last cast its beam over troubled waters at the end of October 1986.

SEVEN OTHER WONDERS OF THE YORKSHIRE COAST

1. The Zetland: "Come along brave boys, come along"

HENRY Greathead of South Shields built the first lifeboat, the *Original*, and as its value as a lifesaver was recognised he soon had orders for more. Number 11 on his work-list went to Redcar, where she eventually came to be called *Zetland*.

She went on station more than 200 years ago, but the old boat is still at Redcar, proudly exhibited at the RNLI museum on the Esplanade, the only surviving Greathead lifeboat. Her maker was a Yorkshireman, born at Richmond in January 1757, and after spending some years at sea he set up as a boatbuilder in South Shields.

In 1789 he responded to an advertisement in the *Newcastle Courant* offering a reward for a plan of a boat capable of saving lives at sea. This had been placed by Nicholas Fairles, a South Shields shipowner, who was the moving force behind a committee of local men intent on forming an "Institution for the Preservation of Life from Shipwreck". Others submitted entries, including William ("Willie") Wouldhave, born in North Shields in 1751, who was described by a contemporary as being noted for "his eccentricity of manners, versatility of mind, and a peculiarly inventive genius".

He died in 1821, and his tombstone, in the churchyard of St Hilda's at South Shields, where he had served as Parish Clerk, proclaimed him "inventor of that invaluable blessing to mankind, the Lifeboat". His model, submitted for the competition, had three main attributes that Willie himself enumerated: "I say it will never sink, nor go to pieces, nor lie bottom up in the water." He had probably heard talk of a coble adapted for lifesaving at Bamburgh, Northumberland, in 1786, by the addition of wide belts of cork round its hull and watertight compartments to add further buoyancy.

Wouldhave was scornful of his rivals, describing Greathead's submission as "a butcher's tray", and claiming it would only float upside down. When the committee held a public examination of the entries and he was not proclaimed winner, Wouldhave stamped out of the room, swearing loudly. Back home, he told his wife he had left his model behind, "and if the Gentlemen have any sense, they will copy that model, because it will save the lives of many sailormen, and that is all the reward I want".

That was exactly what happened. Nicholas Fairles later explained that his committee had commissioned a boat from Greathead's yard that embodied Wouldhave's ideas.

Original, the first lifeboat made to this design, was often spoken of as "Willie Wouldhave's cork boat", and when Henry Greathead asked Fairles for a signed certificate acknowledging him as the inventor of the lifeboat this was refused, although Fairles was happy to credit Greathead with great skill in building the vessels, and his personal addition to Wouldhave's design, a curved keel.

This photograph shows the graceful lines of the Zetland *lifeboat.*

Zetland first arrived in Redcar on 7th October 1802, and quickly proved herself, bringing 15 men safely ashore from two ships wrecked at the mouth of the Tees on 5th December 1802. Seventy-eight eventful and heroic years later, she was last in action at the end of October 1880, rescuing seven men from the German barque *Minna*, which had been swept through Coatham Pier during a storm.

In all, *Zetland* is reckoned to have saved 500 lives. Henry Greathead had built her of seasoned English oak, so her timbers were first hewn some 250 years ago. Despite her age, she looks capable of being put to sea immediately, for she is lovingly cared for by volunteers at the seafront museum.

A small platform affords a view of the boat from stem to stem, for it was part of Greathead's (or Wouldhave'sgenius to give her two prows, so there was no need to turn her round when a rescue had been effected, thus avoiding the risk of going broadside to the breakers. The oarsmen, who sat double-banked, merely faced themselves the other way on their benches, and rowed directly back to shore. To look at this old boat, still equipped with her original oars of Baltic fir, is to marvel at

Redcar teeming with visitors on a sunny day in May 1947. The town's lifeboat is housed on the landward side of the sea front, and launched from the beach. In Victorian times, the boat was manhandled or drawn by horses to a point as close to the wreck as possible, sometimes quite a long haul.

her adventures, and the courage of generations of fishermen who answered the urgent sound of a drum that signalled a launch. The drum is in the museum too, with an effigy of a boy poised as if ready to beat out the summons: "Come along brave boys, come along brave boys, come along, come along, come along".

The *Zetland* was fitted with buoyancy tanks, copper air-boxes round her sides. These were clad in oak to make a seat-like arrangement. If water came aboard, it either escaped through eight drainage holes cut in the bottom of the boat or was baled out. Many fishermen wore bowler hats that had been steeped in tar to make them waterproof, so they also served as scoops.

Lifeboatmen knew she was reliable. An observer wrote in the 1820s that "the boat has been greatly admired by nautical men for its elegance of form; and it is generally considered to be a very good one: indeed, the men who trust their lives to it have great confidence in its capabilities." Their faith was not misplaced, for in all her years of service only one lifeboatman, William Guy, was lost off *Zetland*. On Christmas Day 1836, he was swept to his death while trying to save the crew of a

Danish brig who were clinging to rigging as their ship disintegrated in mountainous seas.

Redcar was rightly proud of Zetland and the men who sailed in her, as the RNLI was to learn in 1864. A new, self-righting boat, provided by John Crossley and Sons, the Halifax carpet manufacturers, was allocated to the town, and the RNLI condemned *Zetland* to be broken up. A hullabaloo ensued, and a call from a crowd of protesters voiced the popular sentiment: "Hold a bit, she's as sound as ivver, and better than new uns." The destruction was halted, and a subscription raised for the old lifeboat's repair.

Lord Stratford de Redcliffe, who was staying with Lord Zetland at Upleatham Hall, got quite carried away and wrote a poem, the quality of which is amply conveyed by the first verse:

> *The Lifeboat, oh! the Lifeboat, we all have known so long,*
> *A refuge for the feeble, the glory of the strong;*
> *Twice thirty years have vanished since first upon the wave*
> *She housed the drowning sailor, and snatched him from the grave.*

This was set to music and published by Boosey and Company, and was no doubt boomed out from stages of Victorian music halls.

The old boat was put in store, but never forgotten, and in 1907 moved into a former lifeboathouse on the Esplanade, which became her permanent home, and where she may be admired today. Further evidence of her place in Redcar's affections came in 1980 when Langbaurgh District Council considered closing the museum. A wonderful row erupted, a "Zetland Lifeboat Savers' Association" was formed, and 5,000 signed a petition. The following year, a solution was reached whereby the RNLI pays a peppercorn rent for the museum, and staffs it with volunteers.

So, after two centuries, *Zetland* is back where she began, in the care of the lifesavers of Redcar, and still serving them well, now as a fund-raiser, and a potent reminder of the gallantry of the men who took her to sea.

2. Filey – the Realisation of a Rich Man's Dream

FILEY's good fortune is that in The Crescent it possesses one of Yorkshire's architectural triumphs, a terrace to rival the finest in Bath. Its centrepiece, Royal Crescent Court, was added in 1853, a magnificent contribution to the development of a resort that had been in progress since 1835.

In that year and the next, John Wilkes Unett, whose family had made a fortune in the Slave Trade, acquired 35 acres to the south of what was then only a fishing village. According to the revised edition of Sir Nikolaus Pevsner's *Yorkshire: York and the East Riding* of 1995*, Unett's plans for this land included elegant houses and hotels as well as the grand terrace.

He was a lawyer based in the Midlands, a man of culture and sensibility who was a co-founder of the Birmingham Society of Arts, and he set an exacting standard for the architects engaged to create his New Filey. As a result, says the new edition of Pevsner, The Crescent "made" Filey,

Taken in the late 19th Century, this photograph explains why The Crescent at Filey is hailed as one of the finest terraces in Britain.

giving the town its distinctive and refined character. It was built over a long period, only being completed in 1890, and consists of six white-stuccoed blocks, all of the quality demanded by Unett.

The fourth from the right, now Royal Crescent Court, was initially Taylor's Crescent Hotel, a prestigious building of four storeys that was essential to Filey's transformation. By 1867 a guidebook was calling the town a "prosperous watering place". Only 30 years before it had been styled "an insignificant fishing village".

The hotel later acquired the pre-fix Royal, a well-deserved honour, for its guest-list resembled an extract from the *Almanac de Gotha*, the Continental equivalent of an aristocratic Who's Who.

At the height of its fame, in the splendid and glittering days of Edwardian England, its visitors were led by "Their Royal Highnesses, the Grand Duke and Duchess of Hesse, Suite and servants".

With them, in the summer of 1910, were "The Hereditary Grand Duke George and Prince Ludwig, Princess Louise of Battenburg and servants, Baron S Massenbach of Darmstadt, and the Baroness G Rotsmann". There were also Yorkshire luminaries: "The Hon Edith Winn, Nostell Priory, Wakefield, the Hon and Mrs GW Winn of Walton Hall, Wakefield, and Sir Algernon F Firth,

Bart, and Lady, of Halifax."

This resounding assembly was catalogued in the town's weekly, the *Filey Post*, whose nominal rolls of visitors were carefully scanned to see who was in town, where they were staying and with whom. Thus was facilitated the graceful business of leaving cards and issuing invitations.

Michael Fearon, the Filey historian, reproduced a selection of the newspaper's lists in his *Old Filey Remembered* (Hutton Press, 1994) and nothing could be more effective in evoking the resort of those days. They even had grand folk in the boarding houses. Lord and Lady Bolton were staying with Mrs Cunningham at No 2 The Crescent. Along at No 12, with Mrs Gibson, were Col and Mrs Starkey from London. For the most part, the buildings on The Crescent are now apartments, including the Royal Crescent Hotel, which closed in 1960. Fortunately their appearance is little changed, and, resplendent in gleaming white paint, they remain what Sir Nikolaus whimsically called "The Brighton part of Filey".

John Wilkes Unett

Unchanged, too, is the panorama that delights the eye from this vantage point. In the foreground are Crescent Gardens, and beyond, changeless yet ever changing, is what Edward Baines in his *Yorkshire* (1822/23) called "a noble bay, abounding with excellent fish", the rocky finger of Filey Brigg tickling it in the ribs.

It was this wonderful prospect that inspired John Wilkes Unett to ensure that his new town was worthy of the view it commanded. He died on 12th November 1856 at Leamington Spa, and is commemorated in the transept of Filey Parish Church, St Oswald's, as "the original projector of New Filey". His latter days were perhaps shrouded in grief, for his gallant son, Lt-Col Thomas Unett of the 12th Regiment of Foot, died in 1855 while leading the British column in an assault on the Redan at Sebastopol in the Crimean War.

Crescent Gardens is another of JW Unett's legacies to Filey, for he insisted that such pleasances were essential to his concept. In glorious bygone summers,. Edwardian gentlemen and their ladies would pay a small entrance fee to stroll there among the clipped lawns and dazzling flower beds ,and listen to an orchestra playing in a bandstand.

By a happy inspiration of Filey Town Council, musicians are now performing in the gardens again. No doubt there are many kind hearts among the people who listen to them, but no longer, alas, any coronets.

* The revised Pevsner (Penguin) is a vast improvement on the origina,l thanks to David Neave, his wife Susan, and John Hutchinson. Other updated editions of the Buildings of England series, including those covering the West and North Ridings, are eagerly awaited.

3. Nature's Kingdom, "a wild roaring place"

WE had gone to Flamborough to explore the headland, assuredly a Yorkshire wonder, and no sooner had we reached the village and set out from Dog and Duck Square than we had a real whiff of the ocean. From an alleyway issued forth as salty a fisherman as ever threw a ninnycock back in the sea. Were we interested in fresh boiled crabs, only £1.50 for three? He deftly bagged our purchase and we went on our way rejoicing.

North Landing is a tidy stride from the village, and the road commands views of caravan sites and hutted camps. But at the end there is ample reward. The White Cliffs of Yorkshire are magnificent. Here the chalk bones that underlie the East Riding Wolds meet the sea, and gradually retreat before its onslaught, though they erode with decorum rather than helter-skelter, like the muddy Holderness shore. The result is that Flamborough Head gets ever beakier.

There are all sorts of colours in the rock above the tidemark, pale green, cream and copper, but white predominates - a startling, brilliant, *impossible* white, the sediment of an ancient sea.

In 1979 the headland became the centrepiece of an area declared Heritage Coast, stretching from Black Cliff Nab at Speeton in the north down to Sewerby Steps near Bridlington. This has brought in its train the establishment of a Heritage Centre at South Landing and the institution of a Heritage Coast Project

Perhaps by reason of this official busybodying, or in total defiance of it, the Headland remains what it has always been – a wild, roaring place where the great battle between sea and land is enacted. At full tide, amid the shrieking of seabirds, waves throw themselves against the chalk, to be repulsed amid soaring plumes of spume and spray. In the end the sea prevails, worrying away at cracks until they become fissures, clawing at the fissures until they become cavities, and opening the cavities into great echoing caves, where the sea surges in at high water, booming in triumph. Its action has sculpted the chalk into wondrous shapes, isolating slim stacks of rock that stand as erect as an umpire's dismissive finger. Elsewhere, small promontories are pierced by exquisitely-worked arches. There are gaping caves like Robin Lythe's (sometimes Lyth's) Hole, supposedly named for a pirate, and handy little coves at North and South Landings, where the coblemen can beach their boats.

We followed a good path round from North Landing. Grass rooted in the boulder clay that overlies the chalk was cropped short and springy. Drifts of wild flowers clung to broken ground at the brink of the cliffs, and butterflies fluttered among clumps of sea thrift. The scents and sounds of summer were everywhere, for the Headland is nature's kingdom, a botanical treasure-house with more than 350 species of plants and ferns, and a nesting-place for as many as 200,000 seabirds.

Flamborough has been drawing the crowds for years. Gordon Home wrote in his book about Yorkshire, published in 1908, that the headland suffered from being popular. He complained that he was "painfully impressed with the feeling that everything bore the tired, unsatisfactory appearance of a place infested with excursionists".

Paths were "overworn", fences "carved with foolish initials", and the noble cape was "littered

These pictures of the North (taken in 1957) and South (1966) Landings at Flamborough provide fascinating studies of the Yorkshire coble, wonderful sea boats of a design that has survived for centuries.

with scraps of dirty paper". Nearly a century on, we found no similar causes for complaint, although it is interesting to speculate on Home's reaction to the changes that have taken place since his visit, not least the line of bungalows strung out across the headland, and the caravans drawn up in ranks. He might have reflected that excursionists, however severe the infestation, did eventually go away, a virtue lacking in bungalows and static caravans.

It might have been worse, too – much worse. In 1938, Lighthouse Farm was sold, and a developer had the brainwave of putting bungalows on its 200 acres. Bridlington Borough Council, which must have been an enlightened body, stepped in, and bought Flamborough Head. General rejoicing ensued, and the Archbishop of York, William Temple, led a service of thanksgiving.

At the time of our visit, the Trinity House lighthouse of 1806, a white-painted brick column 85ft high, was still manned. We responded to a chalked announcement that the next visit would be at 1.30 pm, and were conducted up 119 stairs to the lantern by a gentleman of Trinity House. From this eminence a beam can reach for 29 miles.

Everywhere gleamed. Metalwork shone. Paintwork looked fresh and was in strange lighthousemen's shades of mustardy brown and jade and a kind of chocolate.

From the cast-iron balcony we looked inland, reminding ourselves that the western boundary of Flamborough Parish, girt on three sides by the sea, is yet another wonder, Dane's Dyke. This fortification, two-and-a-half miles long, was an enormous undertaking for primitive people, for an earthen bank stands 18ft high behind a wide ditch. It bears mute testimony to ancient fears of a landward-based attack, and there have been widely differing estimates of its age. One thought is that it was dug out in the 7th or 8th Centuries AD, and we wondered if raiding Vikings settled on the headland, and sought to frustrate any attempt to invade their stronghold by making the huge entrenchment on the landward side.

This is not too wild a fancy. The name Flamborough is derived from Old Norse, and Marie Hartley and Joan Ingilby, writing about the Head in their own *Wonders of Yorkshire* (Dent and Sons Ltd, 1959), averred that the dialect of fishermen there reflected a strong Norse influence.

The place is isolated, by-passed by the main road and the railway. Nobody drops in by accident, and Gordon Home could recall a time when strangers met suspicion, even outright hostility. He told of a visit by the soldier-archaeologist Augustus Henry Lane-Fox Pitt-Rivers in 1879. His main purpose was to excavate trenches across the Dyke, but he also busied himself with a study of the headland folk, who must have humoured their double double-barrelled inquisitor. No fewer than 90 gave "minute particulars" from which the General deduced they were taller than the ordinary run of coast-dwellers, and almost all had dark hair.

Few left the headland. The community was self-sufficient, wary, and content to look within itself for comradeship and marriage partners. They did not, however, exhibit any untoward characteristics.

Another military gentleman of an enquiring turn of mind, Col AH Armytage, recorded in his *Flamborough Village and Headland* that the fisherman would turn back from his boat if on the way to the shore he met a parson, a woman, or a hare, all of which guaranteed ill-luck. Also it was unwise to mention in the presence of a man baiting lines a fox, a pig, an egg, a rabbit, and, once again, the dreaded hare.

The Colonel concluded that this was folly, and it may perhaps have been taken as evidence of in-bred aberration on the part of Flamborians if precisely the same superstitions had not prevailed in any Yorkshire fishing community you care to mention.

Pondering these thoughts, we descended the lighthouse, and placed coins in the cap placed discreetly for the benefit of departing visitors. Then we hurried home to dress our fresh crabs. They yielded perhaps a dessertspoon of meat between them. Young they must have been, and very silly to ignore their elders' advice on the dangers of crab pots. Almost as silly, perhaps, as those expecting a bargain from fishermen landlubbing in ginnels.

* Flamborough Lighthouse was automated in 1996, and the keepers left on 8th May.*

4. The Rock Carvings of Brow Moor

BROW Moor revealed itself as a wonder after ordeal by fire. On 17th September 2003 a small outbreak began on sun-parched Fylingdales Moor, on the landward side of the A171 Whitby-Scarborough road near the Flask Inn. Fanned by a strong wind, a tongue of flame leapt across the highway, spreading the conflagration

It was a prodigious jump. A friend, Harry Green, who served as Bailiff to the Manor of Fyling Court Leet, showed me where it happened. There looked to be 50 yards or so between the charred heather at the western side of the highway, which runs through a cutting at that point, and the singed grass that marked the place where it alighted on the east. The fire raged on across a widening front, engulfing part of Howdale Moor, and blazing seaward across Brow Moor. It only halted at the brink of the old alum quarries on Stoupe Brow because it had run out of moor.

For the people of Robin Hood's Bay and Fylingthorpe it was an extraordinary sight, a line of flames leaping and flaring right across the horizon in a mad dance of destruction.. Billowing smoke darkened the sun, and filled the air with a peaty reek.

This was no ordinary fire, for it not only consumed all the heather and bracken in its path, but also put the peat itself to the flame.

The effect was rather like peeling an orange, for the land, robbed of its protective peat, lay open to the light of day. In places it had been seared down to the pan, the impervious layer that underlies peat moors.

It was in this fashion that Brow Moor revealed its secrets. The area had long been of interest, for occasionally archaeologists had stumbled across carved stones, only for them to disappear again. The lack of landmarks in heather that reached to the far horizon made mapping their precise location difficult.

But what nobody had imagined, or even dreamed of, was the quality and quantity of the evidence of early man on Brow Moor. Here was a wonder indeed for the archaeologists as they trudged through the ash in a systematic search of the headland, first a score of finds, then hundreds, and finally upwards of 2,000.

Before the fire, 17 carved stones had been identified on Fylingdales Moor. Now they were being found in large numbers in the small section of that tract that had been stripped in the fire.

Then there was partially revealed the greatest wonder of all, the Brow Moor treasure, a slab of sandstone incised with a complex geometric pattern. Plainly it would have been of the utmost significance to the men who chipped out this strange symbol with their primitive tools, but nobody today really knows what it means.

All sorts of ideas have been floated. It might represent the sun or the moon, or clouds and birds, perhaps a range of hills. Two experts on ancient rock art, Alan Walker and Brian Smith, argued that it depicted the three elements of the Bronze Age cosmos - the world of the living, the passage to the underworld, and the realm of the dead. Perhaps it was part of a standing stone; perhaps it broke away from a larger slab – who knows?

What is certain is that it is a wonderfully intriguing object, and even in the form of a replica arouses speculation about the kind of people who inhabited the uplands 2,000 years ago. They are shrouded in the mists of prehistory, mysterious folk who carved cup and ring marks into stones, and who perhaps tried farming, for a few patches of bare land bore marks which might have signified ploughing.

They would not have felt exposed, for in those days the North Riding was thick with trees. The most outstanding evidence of the folk who lived among them, perhaps in small clearances, are burial mounds scattered across the moors These were mostly ripped apart in the 19th Century, and vital archaeological evidence either missed, destroyed or dissipated. Some beakers from Fylingdales Moor ended up in a Liverpool museum, only to be destroyed in the Blitz.

Evidence of later activity on the moor also abounded. The Stoupe Brow alum works that started in 1752 needed large quantities of water, and channels were created to deliver supplies. Some run with water to this day. Peat was carted from Howdale until the 1950s, and diggings still remain.

During the Second World War, troops trained on the moor for D-Day, leaving behind them tank-tracks, foxholes, shell-holes, and cartridge-cases.

In 2007 a travelling exhibition dealing with the fire and its aftermath was set up at the Whitby Literary and Philosophical Society's Museum at Pannett Park, Whitby. The centrepiece was a full-scale replica of the great carved stone. The Heritage Lottery Fund supported this excellent enterprise, and Blaise Vyner produced an accompanying booklet, *Fylingdales – Wildfire and Archaeology*, which is wonderfully informative and well illustrated. The whole devastated area falls within the area of common land served by The Manor of Fyling Court Leet, and the Lord of the Manor, Sir Frederic Strickland-Constable, speculated in a foreword on the time it would take to rebuild the peat layer that was so rapidly destroyed.

He added: "It may look as though all is covered up with a nice spread of grass and heather, but we are still a very long way from restoring the heather moor that was there before the fire."

No doubt over the years the moor will renew its shroud, and its wonders will be hidden. But it has been stripped of its secrets, which have been recorded in detail, and made available to those fascinated by our big empty moors and their lost people.

5. Fighting over Fish – By Proxy

HORNSEA Mere is surely a wonder, being Yorkshire's biggest freshwater lake. It was wonderful in another sense, being the *cause célèbre* in a dispute between two great monastic houses, the Cistercian Abbey of Meaux and St Mary's Abbey at York, a Benedictine community of enormous wealth.

The story goes that in 1260 their dispute about fishing rights was settled by combat. The Abbots did not actually do the fighting, but were represented by champions. It is tempting to think it was all carried out properly, with gallant knights on prancing chargers, fair damsels, emblazoned tents, and all the panoply that Hollywood has taught us to associate with jousting and the lists.

Surely, too, it was an event much favoured by the populace, who would turn out for the rough and tumble in the same way we flocked to Roses cricket matches when Yorkshire fielded a team of Yorkshiremen.

Alas, there is no reference to this affair in the most accessible version of the Monastic records, notes published by the Yorkshire Archaeological Society in its Record Series in 1895 and 1931. It is mentioned in Black's *Guide* (1867) and Gordon Home's *Yorkshire* (1908), authorities whom I have no doubt proper historians will regard with suspicion, if not outright disdain.

More acceptable, perhaps, is George Poulson, whose *The History and Antiquities of the Seigniory of Holderness* appeared in 1840/41. The trouble apparently blew up when Meaux sought to establish fishing rights over those parts of the Mere that it claimed lay in its Manors of Seaton and Wassand. St Mary's was firm in its resistance, having been granted the Manor of Hornsea by William the Conqueror's brother-in-law, Odo, Count of Champagne, and having fished the lake since then.

According to Poulson, the legal argument was settled by two trials-by-combat at York. Simon de Warwick, the Abbot of St Mary's, and William de Driffield, his counterpart at Meaux, each hired champions, and, in the words of an authority quoted by Poulson, the parties and their representatives appeared "properly accoutred". The fight lasted "from morning until the evening, when the champions of the plaintiff (Meaux) were beaten to the ground."

The East Riding abbey seems to have fared no better in the second encounter, for Marie Hartley and Joan Ingilby recorded in their *Wonders of Yorkshire* (JM Dent, 1959) that in 1254 Meaux Abbey forfeited all its fishing rights to St Mary's.

The Mere, of 467 acres and up to 11ft or 12ft in depth, is only 12ft above sea level, and less than a mile from the shore. The sea has advanced on it rapidly, and a spire on Hornsea's Parish Church of St Nicholas that collapsed in the 18th Century is said by Poulson to have borne the inscription:

Hornsea steeple, when I built thee,
Thou wast ten miles off Burlington,
Ten miles off Beverley, ten miles off sea.

The Mere attracts much wildlife, and Nature Conservancy has declared it a Special Protection Area. It is thronged with the greedy and messy Canada Geese, and masses of other birds, including warblers and little grebes that nest in the reed beds fringing the water. Beneath the surface lurk many fish, and some whoppers have been caught, including a 27lb pike and a roach of 2lb 13oz. According to Marie Hartley and Joan Ingilby, the Vicar of Foston and his curate undertook a murderous expedition on 4th March 1884, and landed 36 big pike.

The lake occupies a hollow left after the last Ice Age, and if Global Warming causes sea levels to rise, its days as an independent stretch of freshwater may be numbered.

6. Commander Hill and the Coblemen

THE sturdy boats known as cobles have been used inshore by generations of fishermen. They are commonplace on the coast, but a wonder for all that, wonderfully simple, wonderfully safe, and wonderfully effective.

One man devoted himself to finding out all about cobles from the men who built and sailed them. He was Cdr H Oliver Hill, Royal Navy, and it is due to his diligence that much information has been preserved that would otherwise have been lost.

His technique was to communicate with as many coblemen as possible. He did this by letter, recording the information they sent in a journal that built up into a formidable archive. Some of his correspondents were extraordinarily prolific with information, TH Hutchinson of Bridlington supplying no fewer than 65 journal entries. Others who gave ample help were G. Waller of Filey (23), and another Filey man, T. Jenkinson (13). Some dealt with specialised subjects, and it was Dennis Emmerson of Flamborough who enabled Cdr Hill to sketch the fishing gear used in cobles.

He began collecting information in 1953, and continued until his death in May 1973, a period that spanned the abandonment of sail in favour of diesel power. His work, amounting to 200 pages of text and sketches, and 140 photographs, was entrusted to the National Maritime Museum at Greenwich.

This archive was edited for publication by another retired Royal Navy officer, Cdr JEG McKee, and the result appeared in print in 1978 in the Museum's Maritime Monographs and Reports series, entitled *The English Coble*.

It is a triumph, a joy to read. The very name of these ancient craft is a wonder, for it appears in the Lindisfarne Gospels. In about 960AD a Northumbrian monk, Alfred, inserted a translation into the Latin text. St Matthew tells us that Jesus was sailing with his disciples when a storm blew up. They were alarmed, and Jesus said to them: "Why are ye fearful, O ye of little faith?" He then rebuked the winds and the sea, and there was a great calm.

In his version of this passage, Alfred described the vessel in which Our Lord worked the miracle as a couple, using a homely term he could expect to be understood along the coasts of Northumbria and Yorkshire. The Oxford English Dictionary offers *cobyll* in a Chartulary of 1493,

Cobles drawn up at Flamborough in 1961.

and "a coble called the *Margarete*" in a Yorkshire will of 1507.

Although there were variations according to the whims of their builders, the cobles' basic design varied little over the centuries. They are flat-bottomed, clinker-built boats, steered from aft by a long rudder protruding four or five feet deeper into the water than the square stern. Before the internal combustion engine came along, they were propelled by a lugsail and three pairs of oars.

During the 20 years Cdr Hill spent studying cobles they were still being built in quantity along the coast. He found that the craftsmen put them together "by skeg o't ee", without the aid of models, drawings or moulds. He also discovered that master-builders were reluctant to pass on the mysteries of their craft, even to their own apprentices.

The Clarksons at Whitby, the Pounders at Hartlepool, the Siddalls at Bridlington, and the Lavericks at Staithes were all builders of excellent reputation, but the Hopwoods of Flamborough had perhaps the most renowned name south of the Tees. The last of them, "Arg" Hopwood, was to become almost legendary. He worked single-handed, only seeking help when the boats required keeling over. All he needed by way of tools were an adze, a plane, a chisel and a hammer, and he liked to practise his art behind closed doors.

Such men tended to be concerned for the well-being of the boats they created. A Whitby builder, hearing that a boat from his yard was going to Filey, protested: "That's no way to treat a coble", no doubt thinking about the stresses and strains imposed on his handiwork's timbers by the process of landing her on the beach. Much better, he must have thought, for her to have a nice harbour to float in, as at Whitby.

At one time, a coble's home port could be identified by the colour of the paint in which it was finished, red and brown for Flamborough, red and green for Whitby and blue and white or yellow for Staithes. This tradition seems to have died out, and Dora Walker, whose coble *Good Faith* was built by Frank Clarkson in Whitby in 1933, makes no mention of it in her *They Labour Mightily* (Brown and Son, 1947).

Cdr. Hill won the interest and support of the Yorkshire coblemen, and was so warmly received into their company that he knew many by their nicknames, like "Baltic" Boynton and "Lappy" Jenkinson. It was "Lappy" who, in 1972, sent him a comprehensive guide, listing such names as "Welsher", "Cush and Crow", "Soldier Laddy", "Cocky O!", "Ranter Robin", "Peter Jack", "Awd Slep", "Awd Smack", "Young Tab" and "Old Tab".

He was also carefully instructed on signs of ill-luck, like a woman in a white apron, or three seagulls flying together. There were things to avoid, too, like shooting a gull, mentioning pigs or foxes, and whistling on board. The old Navy man was advised not to wind wool by moonlight, as that would put a sailor overboard. He was warned that dreaming of cows bawling at a funeral was an unfortunate portend. However, a black cat crossing his path or the sight of a hunchback might offset bad luck.

Cdr Hill diligently recorded all this in his journal, probably to his own amusement, and certainly to the delight of any reader interested in the Yorkshire coast, and the men who wrested a living from the North Sea.

7. Sermons in Stones – the Dinosaur Coast

NO doubt calling the Yorkshire shore the Dinosaur Coast was a good wheeze for attracting tourists, but it is to be hoped not too many children expect a tyrannosaurus rex behind every nab, and a brontosaurus on the scaur.

It might more accurately have been styled the Ammonite Coast or the Belemnite Coast, for the fossils of these strange creatures, known respectively as snakestones and devil's thunderbolts, abound in the cliffs.

Beyond question though, this wonder is a paradise for geologists. It is easily forgotten that theirs is a comparatively new science. William Smith, who is proclaimed its father, died aged 70 in 1839, by which time the Victorian Age had begun. Smith spent what he called "the calmest and happiest years of his life" in Yorkshire, having had his own first overview of the county from the roof of York Minister. In much the same way as stout Cortez and his men stared across the Pacific from their peak in Darien, he looked towards the coast, but there was no wild surmise about his pronouncement that chalk lay beneath the green hills of the Wolds. He deduced from their contours that they were underlain by the same rock that shaped the Downs of southern England, which he knew well.

He settled in Scarborough in 1824, nine years after the publication of his master-work, the *Geological Map of England and Wales with part of Scotland*, an immense concept that was also large in realisation, being eight-and-a-half feet wide and six feet high. Smith followed this with 21 geological maps of English counties. His classification of the rocks of north-east Yorkshire was wonderfully clear and accurate, "a monument to his genius", as Thomas Sheppard, joint editor of *The Naturalist*, wrote nearly a century later in 1907.

From 1824 to 1834 Smith was steward to Sir John Johnstone of Hackness, Scarborough, one of the prime movers behind the foundation in 1827 of the Scarborough Philosophical Society.

This was the body responsible for building the town's extraordinary Rotunda Museum, a wonder in its own right. Smith, whose bust looks benignly down on visitors, proposed its circular shape "as being more capable of exhibiting, in one simple and intelligible form, the stratification of the rocks of Great Britain". Inner walls were lined with shelves, each of which was used to exhibit fossils of a specific stratum.

The height reached by the shelving was such that it was impossible to make a close inspection of the contents of the upper levels from the floor, a disadvantage eliminated in 1838 when the Society paid James Thompson £6 10s to construct the Museum's oddest feature.

This is a raised platform mounted on four wheels, the inner pair of which run on an iron rail parallel with the wall. By turning a handle – or, more likely, asking an attendant to do the cranking – sages viewing the exhibits stored aloft could be propelled around the room, the power generated by the handle being transmitted to the wheels by an ingenious system of gears.

A frieze depicted a geological profile of the Yorkshire coast from Tees to Humber. Generations of students must have turned dizzy studying this mural, a small hardship to suffer in honour of the father of their science.

While Smith was happily scrambling over the Yorkshire cliffs, which amply confirmed his theory that fossils could be used to identify strata, a young woman at the other end of the country was starting the process which ensured that the shore of parts of Devon and Dorset, could many years later, claim the title Jurassic Coast, and achieve World Heritage status. Mary Anning, born in Lyme Regis in 1799, was only ten when she and her brother discovered the fossilised remains of an 18ft ichthyosaurus, and thereby became famous.

Smith and other pioneers knew that the cliffs of the North and East Ridings contained similar strata to those explored by the young Annings. Indeed, Yorkshire alum workings had yielded finds long before the precocious Miss Anning laid hand to trowel.

In the *Gentleman's Magazine* for October 1760 there was a drawing of "The Skelton of an Allegator found in the Allom Rock near Whitby". The Whitby Literary and. Philosophical Society was formed in 1823, and in the following year paid Brown Marshall £7 for what it called "our estimable fossil". This was claimed to be the most perfect specimen known of a "fossil crocodile, Teleosaurus Chapmani", and the society exhibited it to the public. It can still be seen at the magnificent and recently extended Pannett Park Museum..

Brown Marshall, who found the fossil at Saltwick, was a well-known fossil collector and dealer, for there was already a market for discoveries made in the cliffs. Quarrymen in the East Riding had a sideline in large black lizard teeth, having discovered that savants would untrouser good money for such objects. Villagers round Flamborough Head could usually offer a fossilised sponge, often described by the vendor as "the last decent specimen". Ammonites were for sale in

Whitby, sometimes fitted with crudely carved heads. At one time very large belemnites were collected near Speeton, but by the early 20th Century they were rare, although a villager might dispose of "his last one" at what he considered a fair price.

Meanwhile, students engaged in the new science of geology were beginning to publish books. George Young and John Bird produced a *Geological Survey of the Yorkshire Coast* in 1822, and in 1829 John Phillips, Smith's nephew, who was to become Professor of Geology at Oxford, produced *A Description of the Strata and Organic Remains of the Yorkshire Coast.*

There were plenty of exciting new finds. Quarrying in the Tabular Hills exposed huge masses of coral, a beautiful reef marooned high above Scarborough. A cutting being made for the Hull-Barnsley Railway near South Cave yielded the fossil of one of the four paddle-like limbs used for propulsion by a plesiosaurus, and more belemnites. The remains of a huge lizard were found in a brick pit in the same district. No dinosaurs have been discovered yet, but they passed this way, for the footprints of a three-toed creature that stood on its hind legs have been found imprinted in the scaur north of Scarborough.

Not all discoveries were so ancient. Some date only from after the last Ice Age, which is as yesterday compared with the age of the fossils. Excavations near Sewerby in 1887-88 by CW Lamplugh, a noted geologist, turned up the bones of elephant, hippopotamus, rhinoceros, bison, deer and hyena. A 14-inch mammoth tooth was dug from a gravel pit at Burstwick. The antler of a red deer, found just offshore at Withernsea where it was resting in a peat bed, was hung on the wall of the town's Spread Eagle inn. It had been recovered from what was once the bottom of a freshwater lake, Withernsea Mere, long overwhelmed by the encroaching sea. Other finds there included the near-complete skeleton of a beaver. A bone identified as belonging to a lion was reclaimed from peat near Horsea Mere.

Gravel diggings on Kelsey Hill in Holderness disclosed the fossilised remains of a walrus, then (and perhaps now) the only find of its kind in the country. It was lost for some 20 years, but came to light again when a cellar at Hull Museum was being cleared out. This was recorded by Thomas Sheppard in his *Geological Rambles in East Yorkshire* (Brown and Sons, 1907), perhaps ruefully, for among his many other important offices he was curator of the Municipal Museum, Hull.

Mr Sheppard suggested taking a sledgehammer along when searching for fossils, but this does not appeal to modern geologists, who recommend sorting through rock debris on the beach rather than doing violence to likely rocks.

Contemplating the marine fossils can be a salutary experience. According to the latest studies, the life-forms they represent occupied the earth over varying periods during 30,000,000 years, starting from about 185,000,000 years ago, an almost inconceivable time span. They lived, they died, they sank to the bottom of seas or muddy bays, and they fossilised. There is barely a layer of the strata that does not offer evidence of boundless life. Now is the time for mankind to inhabit the planet, to pillage it and pollute it. Who knows – one day our civilisation, too, may only remain as fragments in a thin layer of earth pressurised into rock, over a space of time so long that it is beyond imagining.

Now that really is something to wonder at.

EPILOGUE –
THE STORY OF MARK WALLACE

The story of Mark Wallace makes a fitting tribute for those Yorkshiremen who went to sea in the days of sail, and who, in many cases, were destined never to see their homes again.

A PACKET of letters that turned up at a house clearance auction in Yorkshire threw light on the little-known world of a ship's boy in the days of sail.

They were written by a lad called Mark Wallace, whose life ended accidentally when he was drowned on 8th June, 1860 while his ship, a merchantman called

Lady Wharncliffe, lay at anchor off the island of Mauritius in the Indian Ocean.

Subsequently, an official return, drawn up according to the requirements of the Merchant Shipping Act of 1856, was sent to his father at Baldersby, Thirsk.

It was from the Marine Department of the Board of Trade, and was included with Mark's letters. It showed he was paid £3 for his first year as an apprentice, £4 for his second, and for the part of the third year, which ended with his death, £1. This represented: "two months and 12 days at £5 per annum as per indentures". Shipowners were only required to pay sailors up to the time of their death. After that, nothing.

Mark had joined *Lady Wharncliffe* on 27th April, 1858, aged 14. His birth was not registered, as that was not a legal obligation then, but he was baptised on 10th September, 1843 at Burton Agnes in the East Riding. He was still living there with his parents at the time of the 1851 census, which gave his age as seven and listed his father, William Wallace, as an agricultural labourer.

The lad completed one voyage on *Lady Wharncliffe*, and was unable to find the time or the money to visit his parents when she returned to the Thames, remaining aboard until she sailed again. It was on this second voyage, to South Africa and the Far East, that he died.

Mark Wallace wrote with a fair hand and was a good speller, attributes that were probably owed to the village school at Burton Agnes. Unfortunately, his letters are not fully dated, but one relates to the days after he joined the ship at Deptford:

"I have being (sic) very much unsettled but I think I am coming round. Now I was in a hole where they keep coals and I began to cry, so I knelt down and offered a prayer to God, and found great relief. I was bound yesterday. The Captain took me to the Counting House, expecting to see me home (i.e. back aboard Lady Wharncliffe)) about two o'clock, and it was three o'clock when Mr Smith came to bind me, so it was four o'clock when I got on board ship.

I hailed the ship ever so many times, and no-one brought the boat, so I was obliged to pay a man 3d to take me over what was only about 30 yards.

There is one boy about 20. The sailmaker told me to tell you he would make sure all my clothes were washed, and if he had any canvas spare he would make me an old smok (sic) to do all the dirty

work and we have a passenger woman who said if I had any little thing to mend, she would do it for nothing. From your very affec. Son Mark Wallace."

The next letter is from Simon's Bay at the Cape of Good Hope, South Africa, and appears to be dated 9th July, 1858, although the last digit is near-illegible. Mark asks his parents to *"give my very best respects to all at the Vicarage especially Mr Calverly"*. He goes on to say some boots he had got at Hull were completely worn out, and he had been obliged to buy a new pair. They cost 13 shillings, and Mark thought them dear, which is hardly surprising, as his wage for the year was only 60 shillings.

He ended that letter warmly: *"Give my best love to Dear Brother David, Grandmother, Aunt Eliza, and dear little sister and accept the same yourselves."*

He also expressed the hope that the *Lady Wharncliffe* would reach St Katherine's Dock, London, *"this day four months"*, and it was from there on 8th January, 1859 that Mark addressed his *"Dear Parents"*:

"I have seen Mr Smith (presumably the representative of the shipowners who bound him apprentice) and asked if I might come home for a few days, and he said that as I only had £3 for the first year it would take all of that to get what clothes I want, but if you liked to pay my passage up and down, he (Mr Smith) said I might come home. The Custom House Officer who belongs to Scarborough told me I could get down for six shillings. He said it would cost me 2s from London to Hull, 2s from Hull to York and 2s from York to Sessay."

In this letter, Mark told his mother and father (who had moved from Burton Agnes to Baldersby) that his apprenticeship was of six years' duration, during which he would receive a total of £35.

Poor Mark was not destined to see his parents and his dearly loved sister and brother during *Lady Wharncliffe's* stay in port, or indeed ever again, for he wrote four days later to say Mr Smith had said he could only have a week off, and, a steamboat trip to Scarborough would take too long, *"therefore Dear Parents I have reconciled myself to stay aboard"*. He asked them to tell Hannah to send him sugar plums, and Mary Ann's *"plum pudden"*, and added further requests, including a towel *"as I have not got one to dry myself"*, two or three pounds of soap, a pork pie, and *"Dear Mother, please to send me a bit of soft bred (sic) and soft butter. I have not got anything but biscuit and salt butter"*. Further pleas were for *"my Bible that Aunt Fanny gave me"*, a bit of India rubber, a silk neck handkerchief, and two or three pocket handkerchiefs *"as I have a bad cold and my nose is always running"*.

Mark went on: *"Tell dear M. A. (his sister Mary Ann) that Miss Hooper told me M.A. was making a purse for me, tell her to send it to me, and as many books as she and dear Sister Emma and you my Dear Parents can muster."*

Sister Mary Ann got a letter too, asking her to make up a parcel with the things he had requested from his parents, plus a comb and brush, a few stamps, a cap *"with those things that lap down over the ears"*, and the little grey jacket *"that I used to wear to go to school on Sunday – the one Miss Hooper gave me"*. He would also be obliged for a little jar of preserve and, as an afterthought, a little ink in a bottle. He winds up by sending Mary Ann his best love and *"the sweetest of kisses"*.

The response to his catalogue of requests appears to have been wholehearted, for there followed an ecstatic letter in which Mark thanked his family for their gifts. He sought advice from his mother on how long her butter would keep, and told of sharing the pork pie with the ship's mate. His cap fitted him very well, and he was grateful for the mittens. He thanked Mary Ann and his mother for the locks of hair they sent him, and in his mother's case: *"I can see your hair is growing grey - when you write again will you tell me if you are so ill at times as you were when I was at home."*

Mark's ship, the *Lady Wharncliffe*, was built at Sunderland in 1854 in the yard of Thomas Stonehouse, who turned out a couple of similar vessels every year. Lloyd's Register for 1856 listed her classification as A1. She was of 428 tons burthen, and registered in London. The owners were given as Smith and Co, which suggests that the Mr Smith who bound Mark apprentice, and advised him on the possibility of getting home between voyages, was the owner or part-owner of the vessel.

In another letter home, Mark tells his family about her: *"My ship is a barque, three masts, and carries about 15 hands every voyage. Sometimes one of the hands will go away in the ship again, but that is very seldom. On board now there is only me, the other boy, the boatswain, the carpenter and the Captain. I think the Captain is going down home to Scarborough. The carpenter also belongs to Scarborough. He knows my Uncle William Garton and my Aunt Fanny very well."*

Mark later informed his parents that his ship was bound for the Cape with Government stores, having taken cargo on board at Deptford. He asked his parent to tell Mary Ann that *"when I received her little note I had kept any tears in for such a long time that I could not keep them in any longer, and I burst out crying"*.

He comes across as a warm and loving lad, devoted to his family and especially Mary Ann. He makes little of the hardships of shipboard life, although he does refer to a week's homesickness at the start of a voyage, and to being obliged to clean the mate's shoes, and to the ill-behaviour of the other ship's boy, who damaged beyond repair the back of a book sent by Mary Ann.

In June 1859, *Lady Wharncliffe* was in Table Bay at the Cape of Good Hope, loading 60 horses for Bombay. He wrote promising Mary Ann a gift, and suggested that Hannah (a servant or friend) should learn the song "Hark to the Bells" to sing to him on his next visit home. In return he said he had *"a great many sea-songs to sing"*.

By October 1859 he was writing from Bombay with news that *Lady Wharncliffe* was bound for Wampoo, China, with a cargo of cotton, and he hoped they would be coming back to England from there, *"indeed, I am sure we shall, as the Captain says he will not accept any cargo except one homeward-bound."*

This letter contains the first hint that all might not be well at home, for, asking his parents to tell Mary Ann of the profusion of green parrots in Bombay, he went on to say how sorry he was to hear that *"dear M.A. was so much weaker"*. He added: *"I so seriously long to see her and you, so I hope the next time you write, you will be able to send me news of her getting better."*

It was not to be. Mark began a letter from Singapore dated 3rd April, 1860 in a conventional way: *"My Dear Parents, I now take the opportunity of writing to inform you that I am in good health and I sincerely hope you are the same…"*

But he went on: *"I was very sorry to hear of My Dear Sister's death. I was eating my dinner and laughing with my other messmates when the steward came and said, here's a letter for you Mark. Ah, that's right, cook, I says, little thinking what was in it."*

He added that as he was writing, one of the boys was playing "Home Sweet Home" on his flute, which must have been hard for him to bear, and indeed the writing paper is stained, as if by tears. Referring to his parents' move to Baldersby, he wrote: *"I shall have no trouble in finding your house when I come home because Father partly told me in your last letter where you lived. He said dear M.A. was buried in Baldersby churchyard near your house."*

He explained that *Lady Wharncliffe* had sailed from China *"all of a sudden"*. She had called at Hong Kong, where they took aboard about 30 Chinese passengers. The ship was now in Singapore loading for Mauritius, which they expected to reach in about three weeks' time. He could not give a firm date for the return home, but he estimated that England was about 13 weeks' sailing time from Mauritius.

This was Mark's last letter home. Within a couple of months, on 6th June, 1860, he was dead.

How this news reached his family in Yorkshire is unknown. The official Board of Trade form, dated 1st September, 1860, was sent in response to an approach by his father, though Mr and Mrs Wallace had to wait until the following year to learn the full circumstances of their son's drowning. On 9th April, 1861, Mrs Wallace's sister, Frances Garton, of 14 Dean Street, Scarborough, (who must have been the Aunt Fanny referred to by Mark) wrote about a call she had made on Captain Joseph Sheader, the master of the *Lady Wharncliffe*, when he came home to Scarborough.

She was told that *"Mark always acted as carpenter's boy, and at the time when the fatal accident occurred, he was carrying a kettle of pitch over a plank laid from the ship to a lighter, where it was to be boiled, it being against the rule to boil it aboard the ship owing I believe to the excessive heat and the danger of fire. Unhappily he lost his balance and fell into the sea beneath. No one was on deck at the time but the carpenter, the captain being in his cabin and the crew in the hold. The carpenter did not see him fall, but heard the splash, and instantly called out that Mark was overboard.*

"Captain Sheader caused the lighter to be moved immediately, fearing he would get beneath it, and then ordered him to be grappled for. Not succeeding in this, he went ashore and fetched a diver. The first time he was dived for proved fruitless, the man went down a second time, and ultimately returned with Mark in his arms. He was taken directly to hospital on shore, where for an hour he was wrapped in blankets, attended by a doctor, and every proper method of restoration employed as usual in such cases, but in spite of all endeavours, he remained without animation.

"He was obliged to be interred that night, as in that climate no one is allowed to be kept long. He was placed in a hearse and followed by a clergyman, the doctor, Capt Sheader and a gentleman of Capt Sheader's acquaintance, in a carriage, as head mourners, the ship's crew following behind. The clergyman read the funeral service over him and gave an affecting and beautiful discourse as he was consigned to the tomb. He is laid in a cemetery, a very beautiful place with flowers."

Mark's mother had apparently requested her sister to ask after Mark's Bible and books. Captain Sheader's response was that they were torn, explaining that Mark had lent them to the whole crew, and they had become dilapidated. However, Mrs Sheader, the captain's wife, was going to London, and if it were possible to recover the remains of the Bible and Mark's other books, she would bring them back to Yorkshire with her.

Before Mrs Garton's intervention, information reaching the Wallaces through official channels had been sparse. The Board of Trade form merely listed Mark was "drowned" and indicated that the net result of his time at sea was £2.2s 11d after deductions. This included 14s raised by auctioning his few belongings among the crew: rug (eight pence), blanket (a shilling), four pairs of trousers (3s), reefing jacket (5s), two pairs of drawers (1s), blue shirt (9d), jumper (7d), book (6d), chest (1s), shoes (6d). Six days after the form's arrival, Mr and Mrs Wallace received a further communication from the Board of Trade, telling them they could collect Mark's wages and effects from the shipping master at Hull.

With that they had to be content. They raised a gravestone in Baldersby St James churchyard to commemorate Mary Ann, who died aged 22 on 16th November, 1859, the cause on her death certificate being given as "hysteria five years" and "phthisis two years" (a form of consumption). In 1868 her father, William Wallace, was buried alongside her, having died at the age of 55. He had progressed to farming on his own account, and his grave is marked by a wooden cross, possibly carved by his surviving son, David, who was a carpenter by trade. Ann Wallace stayed on at Baldersby, and in the 1871 census was listed as a cow-keeper with 17 acres. She lived into the 20th Century, dying, aged 90, in 1904.

For all those years she had kept the letters of her beloved son, and presumably they were passed on through the family. Now they have been knocked down at auction among other odds and ends, emerging as a poignant memorial to a fine young man.

ACKNOWLEDGEMENTS

Yorkshire Post photographs form the core of this book, and represent the work of photographers over many years. Their determination to get the best shot, however challenging the circumstances, has created a wonderful record of our great county. I had the pleasure of working with some of them, including Wilbur Wright, George Stott, Harry Fletcher, Irving Crawford and Terry Carrott, all of whom are represented in these pages, and I am grateful to Peter Charlton, the *Yorkshire Post* editor, for permission to reproduce their work.

The text is derived from more than half a century of writing and reading about Yorkshire, and I have drawn heavily on my collection of books, pictures and newspaper cuttings. Some sources are named in the book, but it would be impossible to list them all. I am indebted to good friends Myra and Peter Smith for the loan of the Mark Wallace letters featured in this last chapter. Saddly, Peter died while this book was being prepared. Thanks also for Humber tug memories to Walter and Dorothy Richardson.

My gratitude, too, to David Joy of Great Northern Books, who offered support and encouragement throughout. My wife, as always, checked the text with the utmost diligence. Without her, the book would be in a mess, and so would I.

INDEX